Female Leadership

Navigate the minefield of modern life to
become a fearless & confident leader.

Sophie Lawrence

Copyright © Sophie Lawrence Publishing

Table of Contents

It's A New World

The fact that there are currently fewer female leaders than there are male ones is universally accepted. It's a situation that is slowly but surely changing, yet there's still a long way to go before the glass ceiling is shattered. Overt gender discrimination is becoming fairly rare, but discrimination nevertheless does still exists.

When you look at North American Fortune 500 companies, only around 6% of them are led by women. Yet 47% of the US working population are women, so why the enormous disparity?
Luckily though, things have been shifting for a long time in favor of a more equal gender balance for female leadership roles within workplaces.

Women are no longer content to sit back and accept unequal status, and there are hundreds of successful female leaders and entrepreneurs paving the way. If you're a woman who aspires to lead or to pursue entrepreneurship, then there's never been a better time to start.

If you're a business looking to increase the gender balance of leaders in your organization, then this book will explain why increasing the number of female leaders can bring more success and profitability. We'll also look at how you can encourage changes to allow more women opportunities to perform in top positions.

Leadership is about ability, not gender, but many inherent feminine traits lend themselves particularly well to leadership. In this book, we'll also explore how women can capitalize on their inherent feminine abilities to improve their leadership potential. We'll go against advising women to embrace more masculine qualities, that may not come naturally, and instead will seek to challenge the view that great leadership requires more than the traditionally viewed masculine traits. Instead, we'll explore the value of more feminine leadership styles and champion their use by women. We'll investigate the barriers you many come up against and explore how you can best overcome them.

In this book, we'll also investigate how employing and nurturing more female leaders can help businesses grow. There are numerous studies that show how women leaders are intrinsic to success. Having a blend of management styles across a business can make your business stronger in the long run. Over the course of the next nine chapters, we'll explore in further detail exactly what women bring to the table, and why we are so damn valuable.

Chapter 1 – The Key to Modern Female Leadership

"It's about knowing yourself and what you're good at. Females, males – anyone can be anything they want to be."
Payal Kadakia, Founder & Executive Chairman of ClassPass

Leadership In Context

For just one small word, leadership encompasses numerous ideas and values. The dictionary definition is the action of leading a group of people or an organization. However, real leadership goes way beyond that simple definition. And often what it means to lead is open to individual interpretation.

In a business context, leadership is how well senior managers in the organization set challenging goals, and inspire and motivate their people to achieve those goals. It's the way they drive the performance of the business to the highest levels possible. It's also how the management teams embody the company's vision and values, and how they motivate and inspire their employees to embody them.

When a business performs well, hits targets, and is level with or ahead of its competitors, this is down to good leadership. Poor performance correspondingly is usually a result of poor leadership. This is why you'll often see a change in leadership shortly after a business announces poor performance figures. Leadership sets the direction a company is headed in and then steers it towards that direction.

Awesome Female Leadership

Meg Whitman joined eBay in 1998 as CEO. At that time the company employed a total of 30 people and grossed $4,000,000 a year. By the end of 2008, under Whitman's leadership, the company had grown beyond all expectations. eBay now employed 15,000 people and grossed $8,000,000,000. She stepped down as CEO in 2008, but her legacy as an incredibly effective leader is indisputable. 2008 was also the year that she was inducted into the U.S. Business Hall of Fame.

So, what was it about Meg Whitman's leadership that brought eBay from a quirky, mildly successful business to a multi-billion dollar powerhouse?

Whitman gave the business some much-needed direction through her leadership.

She was passionate about putting customers first and transforming eBay's website from 'clunky' and difficult to use, to slick and user-friendly. She reorganized the company, splitting it into twenty-three different business categories and appointing executives to lead each category.

She was determined to set a clear vision and to make sure that everyone in the company understood the vision as well as their part to play in achieving it. She knew that for eBay to reach the success she envisioned, she'd need to have everybody on board.

To do this, Whitman also focused on employee engagement, believing that the best results come from a motivated and happy workforce. Her employees have been known to describe her as *'relentlessly optimistic'* and how they admired her ability to stay focused and positive.

As a result of Whitman's leadership style, employees were more empowered, the business functioned more efficiently, and customer satisfaction increased dramatically. Not to mention, of course, the profits!

Leadership Styles

All business leaders are mostly aiming for the same outcome – high profit and a stable business that can withstand unpredictable outside forces. However, the way they approach it can differ significantly.

There are numerous leadership styles and various models that explore the different ways people approach leadership. It would take an entirely new book to cover them all. So, for the purposes of this chapter, we'll look at a couple of the most common and influential leadership style models.

Lewin's Leadership Styles

One of the earliest studies into leadership styles was led by psychologist Kurt Lewin in 1939. Lewin and his team identified three core leadership styles, that formed a basis for later, more complex leadership theories.

The study involved assigning three groups of schoolchildren to be led by one of the three types of leader: democratic, autocratic, or laissez-faire. The researchers then noted the children's response and performance under the different types of leadership.

These three types of leadership are a common model used in leadership and management courses across the globe. Let's take a closer look at how the three different styles compare:

Autocratic Leadership

Autocratic leaders are authoritarian. They set clear expectations and timelines. Autocratic leadership sets a clear divide between the leader and the followers. In this leadership style, the leader makes all decisions independently, without seeking any input from their followers.

The positives of this style are that employees are given clear instruction and understand what is expected of them. It's useful in situations where deviation from rules and standards can have dramatic consequences. For example, it may be the style of leadership most appropriate to a heavily regulated industry.

The negatives are that it discourages creative thinking, it breeds poor employee engagement, and it can be seen as a very dictatorial style. It can create a very hostile environment when used inappropriately. Also, it can lead to an 'us and them' mentality where employees and leaders appear to be on opposite sides.

Autocratic leadership is generally considered quite an old-fashioned style of leadership that has more limitations than positives. It's a helpful style to adopt in certain situations that need a strong leader to take charge and make decisions, but it's rarely an appropriate style to use every day.

Democratic Leadership

Democratic leaders encourage group participation in activities and two-way discussion. They will often provide guidance and advice but are less likely to provide rigid rules and instructions. They generally value the outcome over the process. Democratic leaders encourage followers to voice their opinions on decisions, but they retain the final say.

By encouraging participation, democratic leaders foster better engagement and more motivated followers. It also allows for more creative thinking and more effective teamwork.

In Lewin's study, this was considered to be the most effective leadership style. Although the children in this group produced less than the children in the Autocratic group, the output was of higher quality.

Laissez-Faire Leadership
Laissez-faire leaders provide very little direction or guidance and encourage followers to make decisions themselves with little or no input from the leader.

In Lewin's study, this group produced the least and had the most trouble both cooperating and working independently. They were also the most demanding of the leader.

Newer Leadership Styles and Models

Those three leadership styles are fairly polarizing, and few leaders fit neatly into those categories all of the time. However, Lewin's work provided a foundation for other studies into leadership theory that has expanded and developed into a variety of leadership styles.

Here are some of the more popular leadership styles that

have been identified.

Transactional Leadership

Transactional leadership is most closely related to Lewin's autocratic leadership style. In this leadership style, the relationship between leader and follower is completely transactional and usually based on financial compensation for tasks completed.

The transactional leader gives clear instructions and sets expectations. Followers are clear on what is expected of them, and what the expected compensation will be. Transactional leaders may offer incentives for high performance as a motivational tool, but they don't tend to recognize employee engagement as necessary or relevant to their organization.

Like autocratic leadership, this leadership style tends to result in less creative thinking. It's a suitable style for leaders in positions where their employees are producing high volumes like in manufacturing, or in high volume sales. It's least suitable for leaders who need their employees to solve complex problems or come up with creative solutions regularly.

Situational Leadership

Situational leadership is a leadership model that encompasses different styles. The basis of this model is that while there are different styles, they should vary by situation and not by the individual. It recognizes that different leadership challenges need different leadership approaches.

One of the most popular models of situational leadership is the *Hersey-Blanchard Model* that identifies four core leadership styles:

Telling – Much like the autocratic style, this is where the leader gives directions and expects them to follow without much question.

Selling – This is where the leader recognizes the need to persuade employees or followers to buy into an idea or vision.

Participating – This is where the leader encourages employees or followers to have an active role in decision making, but the leader remains hands-on and involved.

Delegating – This is like the laissez-faire style, where a leader steps back and allows the group a lot of autonomy over decisions.

The key to this model is that none of these styles are considered superior. They are all better suited to different situations, and a good leader will be able to identify and employ the appropriate style for any given situation.

In this model, the style a leader chooses will depend in part on the 'maturity' level of the employees, along with the task itself. Their 'maturity' level is their knowledge and competence in the role. For employees with low knowledge and competence, a delegating style would be inappropriate for most tasks, as those employees would need a high level of guidance and supervision. For highly skilled and competent employees, one of the more hands-off approaches would be suitable in most cases.

Transformational Leadership
Transformational leadership is a leadership style that is generally considered to be one of the most effective. Transformational leaders are excellent at motivating and

inspiring followers to achieve goals. They are usually energetic and passionate speakers, with high emotional intelligence. They value the individual contributions of their followers and readily offer praise and recognition.

Transformational leaders often take on a coaching and mentoring role with their employees. They look to support and develop the people they lead, nurturing their talents, and placing people in positions that suit their unique strengths.

This style is particularly well-suited to identifying how an organization needs to change and leading them through that change. Considering the fast pace of most industries in this day and age, the ability to lead change effectively is an essential skill for anyone aspiring to a leadership role.

In several studies, this style of leadership has been shown to drive higher staff engagement and higher performance than other styles. Meg Whitman is one example of a leader who embodied a transformational leadership style. In fact, studies have shown that women naturally tend to have a transformational leadership style. Leadership researcher Bernard Bass conducted one of the studies which concluded that women tend to have more characteristics aligned with transformational leadership.
Leadership theory is a thriving subject, and these leadership styles barely scratch the surface of the complex study of leadership. They do, however, provide a good basis for understanding some of the more common styles of leadership.

Vital Lessons from the Past

Although female leadership on the scale we know it today

is fairly new, there have been examples of women in leadership positions all throughout history. Women have led nations, founded religious organizations, built businesses and led social movements. And for most of history, they have done so against incredible odds.

Let's take a look at some of the most notable examples of historical women in leadership.

Cleopatra

Cleopatra is arguably one of the most famous women leaders of all time. Her infamous affairs with Roman leaders Julius Caesar and then later Mark Anthony sometimes overshadow her achievements as the last Pharaoh of Ptolemaic Egypt.

Her father was King Ptolemy XII. After his death, the throne passed to Cleopatra and her ten-year-old brother Ptolemy XIII. Cleopatra was 18 at the time. During this time, Egypt suffered from a poor economy and political turmoil.

Shortly after they ascended the throne, a rift began to appear between Cleopatra and her brother. The differences between them led to Cleopatra fleeing to Syria in order to assemble an army to take back the throne.

Eventually, it was a romantic alliance with Julius Caesar that saw Ptolemy XIII defeated and Cleopatra restored to the throne as Queen. After Caesar's death, Cleopatra was summoned to Rome by Mark Anthony, beginning her second affair with a Roman politician. Cleopatra ruled Egypt for around two decades, but there are few records of her achievements as a ruler. Most historical accounts concentrate on her influence over Roman politicians and not her own country.

It's said that Mark Antony killed himself after being defeated by his rival Octavian, and believing Cleopatra to be dead. When Cleopatra discovered this, she is said to have committed suicide by being bitten by an asp. The location of her burial has never been discovered.

Catherine The Great
Catherine II of Russia, also known as Catherine the Great, was Empress of Russia from 1762 until her death in 1796, and was the country's longest-ruling female leader. She gained the throne following a coup d'état against her unpopular husband Peter III. Catherine herself orchestrated the coup and seized the throne.

Catherine presided over a time of growth and stability for Russia. She modernized Russia, introduced inoculations and established the Smolny Institute for Noble Maidens – the first state-funded higher education institution for girls. She also pushed back against the power the church held within the state and encouraged the development of the economy.

Catherine had a great interest in education and culture. She was a patron of the arts and presided over the Russian Enlightenment. Her rule is often referred to as the Golden Age of Russia.

Queen Elizabeth I
Queen Elizabeth was the daughter of Henry VIII and Anne Boleyn. She ascended to the English throne in 1558, aged 25 after the death of her brother Edward VI.

She remained on the throne until her death in 1603, and reigned over a period of great change and growth. She introduced the first form of welfare in England and famously defeated the Spanish Armada. Elizabeth was also responsible for building on her father's legacy and transforming England into a country of Protestant faith. Her tolerant approach that allowed Puritans and Catholics to continue following their faith earned her a lot of approval. She still faced threats from Catholics however, who wanted to see her Catholic cousin Mary on the throne.

Elizabeth was an intelligent queen with a lot of political savvy. However, she was not without her critics. During her reign, Parliament became more influential, and there was conflict over several issues likes religion, her refusal to marry, and trade monopolies.

Elizabeth's reign is seen as a 'golden age' of English culture when Shakespeare was writing his plays and theatre became popular.

Queen Victoria

Another English Queen, Victoria reigned for 63 years and survived six potential assassination attempts. She was the first Queen to rule from Buckingham Palace and was the longest-serving British monarch until the reign of Elizbeth II. Victoria was Queen during the rapid expansion of the British Empire, and she eventually ruled over the largest empire in history.

She was, for the most part, a Queen who promoted peace and tolerance. Under her rule, all British colonies abolished slavery.

She married her first cousin, Prince Albert in 1840. Initially, Victoria ensured that Albert had no part in governing the country, but over time as she bore nine children, she relented and allowed him a larger political role.

To quell the growing republican movement, Victoria ushered in a new era of a more visible monarchy. She became a patron of numerous charities and made hundreds of civic visits. After Albert's death, however, she withdrew from public life and spent the majority of her time at Balmoral.

She did reemerge into the public eye later, and her Golden and Diamond Jubilees were widely celebrated across the British Empire.

Anna Bissell
When Anna Bissell's husband died in 1889, Anna became the very first female CEO in the United States. She was by all accounts a very effective leader, bringing the Bissell brand of carpet cleaners and vacuums to the international market.

Under her leadership, the company went from strength to strength and reportedly even Queen Victoria insisted on there being a Bissell at Buckingham Palace. By 1899 Bissell was the largest organization of its kind.

Anna Bissell was the embodiment of a transformational leader, implementing labor policies like pension plans before these were the norm.

Eleanor Roosevelt
Eleanor Roosevelt was the first First Lady to take an active political role. Up until President Roosevelt's election, the function of a First Lady was purely social. However, Eleanor had been campaigning on her husband's behalf throughout his political career. She'd also established businesses of her own in a factory to help Hyde Park families supplement their income, and bought and taught in

a girls school.

When her husband was elected, Eleanor was not content to sit back and attend social functions. Instead, she paved the way for future First Ladies by holding press conferences, writing a newspaper column, and supporting civil rights movements, among other activities.

Even after her husband's death, Eleanor continued to have political influence. She campaigned for presidents including John F Kennedy, was appointed as a United Nations delegate, and continued to support civil rights movements.

Indira Gandhi
Indira Gandhi was the first (and, at the time of writing, the only) female Prime Minister of India. She is also the second-longest serving Prime Minister. Gandhi served for several terms but was assassinated by her own bodyguards in October 1984.

Gandhi's introduction to politics began when she served as her father's personal assistant during his own time as Prime Minister. During this time, she was elected as President of the Indian National Congress. After her father's death, she joined the cabinet as Minister of Information and Broadcasting. In 1966 she was elected as Prime Minister of India.

Gandhi took India to war with Pakistan in 1971, and under her leadership, India's armed forces were victorious. That victory led to the creation of Bangladesh, and Gandhi was the first government leader to recognize the new country.

After a challenge from the opposition party that could have seen her banned from politics for six years, Gandhi appealed to the Supreme Courts. When their response was not what she anticipated, she declared a state of emergency throughout India. During this time she assumed emergency powers, imprisoned her opponents and passed several new laws. Many of her measures were highly unpopular and included a mass sterilization drive.

Emergency rule ended in 1977, and along with it, Gandhi's tenure as Prime Minister. In 1980, however, she was re-elected as Prime Minister once more and served until her assassination. Her final term was once again filled with controversy, predominantly over the handling of escalating conflict with Sikh separatists.

Barbara Jordan
Barbara Jordan was both the first woman and the first African-American to deliver a keynote speech at a Democratic National Convention.

Jordan studied political science and history at college, and then went on to graduate law school and passed the bar in 1960. She was inspired to become an attorney in high school after hearing a speech delivered by Edith S. Sampson.

Jordan opened a private law practice in 1960 and later won a seat in the Texas Senate in 1966. She was re-elected to the Texas Senate in 1968 and served until 1972, when she was elected to the House of Representatives. She was the first women elected in her own right to represent Texas in the House.

Perhaps Jordan's most memorable moment was delivering a speech before the U.S. House Judiciary Committee, supporting the impeachment of President Richard Nixon. Her eloquent and intelligent speech is often credited as the reason that Nixon resigned, recognizing that he could not defend the points that Jordan eloquently raised.

Margaret Thatcher
Margaret Thatcher was the first female Prime Minister of the United Kingdom. She was also the longest-serving British Prime Minister of the 20th-century. Thatcher held office for three full terms from 1979 until 1990. She was renowned for her uncompromising leadership style and was commonly known in the press as the 'Iron Lady'.

Thatcher was always a controversial figure in British politics, mostly due to her hardline policies and her drive to privatize national services. Her popularity nosedived during a period of recession and high unemployment, and her financial and anti-unionist policies were frequently met with resistance from the opposition

One of her most controversial actions was the closure of a number of British mines, and her refusal to meet the demands of the miner's union. A year-long miners' strike ensued, and eventually, the union conceded.

During the 1980s, Thatcher was often described as the most powerful woman in the world. In 1999, Time Magazine listed her as one of the most important people of the 20th century.

The Differences in Recognized Female Leadership Roles

While history provides a rich source of evidence that women can successfully lead, female leadership hasn't been taken seriously until more recently. One of the reasons for that is very few women rose to a leadership position in their own right. Most historical female leaders obtained their position from either privilege of birth or privilege of marriage. Often their leadership was controversial in some way, and all the more complicated for them being female.

Cleopatra had a valid claim to the Egyptian throne, but it took an alliance and an affair with a powerful man to secure her position. When the throne was secured, she was, by most non-Western accounts around that time, a great ruler and a keen scholar and scientist. Unfortunately, her actual achievements as a leader are glossed over in historical accounts with her affairs taking center stage over her leadership skills.

For the vast majority of women throughout history, the idea of them being able to hold the kind of positions that were open to men was unthinkable.

Of course, some of the historical barriers to leadership have always been class and not just purely gender. However, the fact remains that even women born to wealthy households for most of history would not have been encouraged to aspire to much beyond becoming a dutiful wife and good mother.

In the list above, Margaret Thatcher stands out as one woman who carved out a highly successful political career on the back of her own achievements. However, it's interesting to note that her leadership style is often described in more masculine terms. More often than not this is in a detrimental tone rather than celebratory of her strengths. She was certainly more of an autocratic leader than a laissez-faire one. It could also be argued that at times she demonstrated traits consistent with a transformational leader, for example, having the vision and ability to pull an entire country through a period of significant change. Factually, she left Britain financially stronger than she found it, regardless of people's opinions on how she achieved that. Something that is not often recognized and celebrated.

The Glass Ceiling

As just explored, historically, there were female leaders but they were the outliers, anomalies and they often faced severe opposition. In the early 20th century, women were still not allowed to vote. And even after gaining the vote in 1920 and getting a boost on the path to equality, leadership positions remained out of reach due to a lack of equal education opportunities.

Women were still denied access to many higher education opportunities, including Ivy League colleges. Getting a degree from a college like Harvard was impossible until 1963. And without access to those opportunities, women were poorly placed to step into leadership positions.

Fortunately, present-day situations are changing, albeit too slowly. A small number, 6% of leaders in Fortune 500 companies are now women but until 1972, when Katherine Graham became CEO of the Washington Post, there were none at all. So, when did thinking start to shift from leadership being a male-only occupation to it being possible for women to be considered?

A lot of this shift in mentality has only happened over the last 100 years.

Even with a good college education, women were only expected to fulfill secretarial and admin roles. Few, if any, corporations would even consider interviewing a woman for a management position or a professional role. The reasoning for this inequality was accepted social gender roles – men should be the breadwinners and women should be looking after the home and children.

It wasn't until the 1970s that these views were challenged and began to shift slightly. The Equal Rights movements influence meant women were no longer explicitly excluded from managerial roles and all professional occupations. However, there were still limits on what they could achieve. Only lower levels of management were attainable, yet, it was a move in the right direction.

The oft-used term 'glass ceiling' to describe the invisible but very real barrier preventing women from accessing higher-level leadership roles, was first used by the Wall Street Journal in 1986.

The concept of the glass ceiling caught on quickly, and eventually US Congress established an investigatory commission specifically for the 'Glass Ceiling' idea. In their report, they noted that the glass ceiling was driven by the notion that women were likely to quit working to start a family. No executives were willing to hire women for important roles because of the possibility that they might start a family.

New laws were passed to prevent the overt exclusion of women from leadership roles. And as a result, over a length of time, we've seen a rise in the number of female leaders in high-level positions. On a positive note for women in the present day, it's now easier than it's ever been for women to rise through the ranks of leadership. Unfortunately, the path to higher levels of leadership for women still isn't as clear as it is for their male counterparts but the situation is progressing at a rapid pace.

It's not true that women are better leaders than men, nor is it true that men are better leaders than women. Ability and talent are determined by many things, such as upbringing, socio-economic background, genetics, education, and environment – NOT GENDER!

However, it is true that men have always been given more opportunities to lead than women have. In the next chapter, we'll look at what, if any, general differences there are between men and women when it comes to leadership. We'll also explore why it is that there still a lack of female leaders in the 21st Century?

Chapter 2 – A Lack of Quality Female Leaders?

"A woman can and should be able to do any political job that a man can do."
Richard M. Nixon, 37th President of the United States.

Women's rights have come a very long way from women being both unable to vote and being unable to hold positions other than secretarial roles. Women serve in armies all over the world; they are business leaders, political leaders, and have the same legal status as any male in the USA.

So why then, are we seeing so few female leaders in the business and political arena? In this chapter, we'll take a look at some of the possible reasons that there's a general lack of female leaders.

Are Men Actually Better Leaders?

One of the reasons that women were initially excluded from leadership positions was the belief that women have a 'temperament' that makes them unsuitable to lead. Even President Nixon, despite the above quote, was heard saying 'off the record' that *"I don't think a woman should be in any government job whatever. I mean, I really don't. The reason why I do is mainly because they are erratic. And emotional. Men are erratic and emotional, too, but the point is a woman is more likely to be."* This coming from a man who was publicly supportive of women's rights makes this comment all the more insulting. It demonstrates how insidious barriers have historically prevented women from achieving their full potential.

As barriers were slowly but surely removed, women began to face a critical issue. To move past this invisible barrier they could either adopt stereotypically masculine behavior or accept that leadership would be out of their reach.

Unfortunately, even this 'solution' of adopting masculine behaviors came with its own set of problems. Women who behaved like men might have been more likely to be considered for leadership positions, but they'd still come under intense scrutiny and criticism for not acting like a woman. Add to this the fact that the behaviors that garner respect and admiration in men can generate distrust and cause a loss of respect when displayed by a woman.

This belief that women have trouble controlling their emotions persists to some extent to this day, although it's no longer such a widespread belief. Women's perceived intrinsic qualities are now more often seen as positive in leadership positions rather than a reason for them to be excluded.

According to 2018 research by Pew, most Americans agree that women are more skilled at encouraging and supporting, while men are considered better at decision-making and problem-solving. The numbers from the Pew research are very illuminating, and unless otherwise specified, it is this research that will be referred to in this chapter.

However, the invisible barriers are still there. Various studies have shown that men are generally taken more seriously at work. When a suggestion is made by a man it tends to be received more positively than if a suggestion is made by a woman. Even when the idea is presented in the same way, using the same language, the men are taken more seriously.

It's worrying that people have a different perception of the same behavior depending on which gender it comes from. When male leaders communicate unpopular decisions like job cuts, it's less likely to make them less popular with employees, who perceive them as effective leaders who make decisions in line with what's necessary for the business. On the other hand, when the same decisions are taken by female employers, they lose their popularity and receive strong criticism, as demonstrating qualities like strength and dominance is unfeminine behavior.

Women who demonstrate more stereotypically feminine behavior, like demonstrating compassion, are more popular but tend to be perceived as less competent. The more competent and strong they look to employees, the less popular they become. For female leaders, it's a catch-22 situation.

In a 1992 review of studies on gender and leadership, it was found that female leaders were usually evaluated as positively as male ones. There was, however, a difference between how women leaders with a more autocratic style were viewed in comparison to male leaders with the same style. The women were much less likely to be viewed positively than the men.

In a later 2008 study of gender differences in transformational and transactional leaders, research participants rated female transformational leaders more positively on extra effort, satisfaction, and effectiveness. In addition, female research participants rated female transformational leaders more positively.

Although there are still people who hold these outdated beliefs about how men are better leaders than women, the facts simply don't support this belief. For example, research by the Peterson Institute for International Economics revealed a correlation between higher profits and the number of women at the 'C-Suite'. Companies with more leadership positions filled by women, had at least 1% higher net profit margin when compared to companies without female leaders.

For example, Apple is one of the top-performing Fortune 500 companies, and it's no coincidence that they also have a comparatively high percentage of women leaders at 29%.

There's plenty of good news about how perspectives are shifting when it comes to gender differences in leadership. The Pew research confirms that the majority of Americans would like to see more women both in top corporate and top political leadership positions. The nationally representative survey of 4,587 adults was conducted online June 19-July 2, 2018.

According to the survey, most people do believe men still have an easier path to the top and that women have to do more to prove their worth. However, it does confirm that Americans largely see men and women as equally capable when it comes to the key qualities and behaviors that are essential for leadership. This even though the majority do believe that men and women in top leadership positions in business and politics do tend to have different leadership styles.

Out of those people who believe men and women have different approaches to leadership, 62% say neither approach is better. For those who feel one gender has a better approach, 22% say women's approach is best, 15% say men have a better approach.

For leadership in both business and politics, most respondents believe that men and women are equally strong in key leadership qualities, but where people see a difference, tends to be the women that they see as stronger in most areas. One key area where people believe women are better than men is in being compassionate and empathetic, and a large number believe women are better at working out compromises and standing up for what they believe in.

Although women have the edge in being seen to demonstrate compassion, this may not be seen as very helpful in their leadership career. 46% of Americans do view compassion as a positive trait for men in politics, however, only 29% say it mostly helps men in business. Instead, nearly half of the public (47%) says being compassionate makes no difference in helping a man get ahead, and 22% say it hurts men in the workplace. The results for women echo this sentiment.

Overall, male leaders are seen as better than female leaders in willingness to take risks and negotiating profitable deals. Compared to compassion and empathy, these are more recognizably useful traits in a leadership position.

When it comes to business leadership, in particular, women have a slight edge in creating a safe and respectful workplace and being honest and ethical. These are also two traits that Americans see as crucial to being a good business leader. For creating a safe and respectful workplace, 43% say women are better, 52% say there is no difference, and only 5% say men are better at this.

And while the majority of respondents say there is no difference between male and female leaders when it comes to valuing people from different backgrounds, considering the impact of business decisions on society, providing guidance and mentorship to young employees, and providing fair pay and good benefits, those who do see a difference tend to believe women are better at these competencies.

Women are much more likely than men to agree that female business leaders are better than their male counterparts at creating a safe and respectful workplace and providing mentorship to young employees. The majority believe that women and men are equally capable of handling key policy areas and running companies across industries.

On the whole, people are positive about the benefits of female leadership. 69% of respondents say that having more women in top positions in business and government would likely improve the quality of life for all Americans. 77% believe more women leaders would improve the quality of life for women specifically. When asked if more women leaders would improve the quality of life for men, 57% agreed it would.

Unsurprisingly, women are more likely than men to agree that more women in top leadership positions would be beneficial overall. Over 65% of women believe having more female leaders would improve the quality of life for men, compared with 47% of men.

When asked whether certain personal characteristics would help or hinder men and women seeking to succeed in business or politics, approximately 70% believed that being assertive and ambitious would help a man's chances in both business and politics. Around half of respondents see assertiveness and ambition as helpful to women who are aiming for top leadership positions. In comparison, about a quarter believe being assertive and ambitious can actually hurt a woman's chances of getting ahead in politics and business.

One attribute that's considered more helpful to women than to men is physical attractiveness. 60% of respondents believe it helps women get ahead in both politics and business.

Openly showing emotion was seen as being more harmful than helpful to both men and women. However, it was seen as more harmful for female leaders than male leaders. 52% say openly showing emotions hurts women in politics, but only 39% say this about men.

Some of these results echo the 2012 leadership research by Zenger and Folkman. More than 7,300 leaders were studied and scored against sixteen identified leadership competencies.

Women scored higher than men on twelve of these competencies, including:

- Takes initiative
- Practices self-development
- Displays high integrity and honesty
- Drives for results
- Develops others
- Inspires and motivates others
- Builds relationships
- Collaboration and teamwork
- Establishes stretch goals
- Champions change
- Solves problems and analyzes issues

- Communicates powerfully and prolifically

Men and women were rated equally in:

- Connects the group to the outside world
- Innovates
- Technical or professional expertise

The only area where men outscored women was in the ability to develop a strategic perspective. Even here, the researchers posited that more senior leaders always score higher on this competency. Because most top-level leaders are male, the aggregate scores favor men. However, when you compare only leaders at the top level, women and men are rated equally.

This survey is particularly interesting as it measured the perspective of leader's employees, peers, and managers. Instead of asking people if they thought women were better than men, they were rating an individual leader that they worked closely with, without overtly considering gender. Women consistently outperformed men in almost every single competency. Even more interesting is the fact that the higher the level of leadership, the more likely it was that women would score higher than their male counterparts.

The evidence is clear – men do not make naturally better leaders.

Unfortunately, despite the evidence to the contrary, even women tend to believe that men are better leaders. According to the Pew research, most women show a preference for male leaders. Even though studies like the Zenger Folkman research consistently demonstrate that male leaders are not more competent than their female colleagues, this leadership gender bias is demonstrated by both men and women.

Differences Between Genders in Leadership

Although men and women are both effective leaders, there are some general differences in typical leadership styles. It's important to stipulate here that not every male leader will be typical, nor every female leader. There are lots of leaders who naturally have a different leadership style than that is typical of their gender and it isn't necessarily because they feel the pressure to adapt their natural behavior.

With that said, here's a breakdown of the key differences that researchers have observed in leadership styles:

<u>Male Leadership Style</u>
Typically, men lean heavily towards a more transactional leadership style. They place a large emphasis on achieving goals. They tend to expect to provide direction and have that direction followed. Each task their employees complete is a transaction that is either successful or unsuccessful and depending on the outcome, employees should be either disciplined or rewarded.

They don't feel compelled to explain most of their decisions, as they don't believe that their employees need anything more than the transactional reward of salary and/or bonuses for motivation. They often take a hands-off approach to leading and keep themselves separate from their teams. This separation can be seen as a positive among employees, who are left to 'get on with it', however, it can become an issue if an employee needs support that the transactional leader is unwilling to provide.

Men value the clarity associated with a strong hierarchical structure and are more likely to enforce hierarchical boundaries. They consider these boundaries necessary to make sure that everyone is clear on their tasks and responsibilities.

Female Leadership Style
Typically, women lean more towards a transformational approach. They also emphasize on achieving key goals, but they take a more involved approach to achieve them. Female leaders are more hands-on with their teams and look for ways to motivate them beyond a transactional system of discipline and reward. They place more emphasis on their team's personal development and tend to provide explanations for their decisions. They are also more likely to consult their team's on decisions and take input from others – making decisions a more collaborative effort. Female leaders provide a higher level of support to their employees and they value teamwork and effective communication.

Transformational leaders have higher performance rates and more engaged employees. Their motivational style encourages creativity, teamwork, and communication. Detractors of the transformational style consider transformational leaders to be too 'soft' and reluctant to tackle poor performance. This, however, is not true. Transformational leaders do still implement disciplinary action where they find it appropriate, but they tend to take a 'will' vs 'skill' approach when deciding what action is appropriate. Poor performers that they believe simply need support to develop skill will be given support and encouragement. However, where employees are seen to be underperforming because of behavior rather than lack of skill, transformational leaders will take disciplinary measures.

Transformational leadership is commonly seen among women leaders. One of the reasons that women are more likely to adopt a transformational leadership style is that it naturally lends itself to feminine traits like compassion and communication. As we've already noted, adopting a more masculine, autocratic approach can backfire for women. A transformational style allows them to leverage their gender's natural strengths.

Female leaders focus more on collaboration and the sharing of ideas across teams and departments. Female leaders are more likely to attribute credit for success to employees, without overemphasizing their own personal contribution. Conversely, when unsuccessful, they are less likely to blame others or put it down to bad luck. Instead, they are more likely to question their own competence.

Women are less likely to enforce hierarchical boundaries. Instead, they take a holistic approach to managing the team environment and pay more attention to ensure they treat every employee fairly.

What Drives The Differences In Leadership Styles Between Genders?

Numerous experts have pointed out that these differences begin in childhood, where societal gender expectations see more boys enrolled in sports teams and encouraged to engage in competitive behavior. Girls are encouraged more towards gentler and creative pursuits like dance.

These stereotypical expectations influence us right through to adulthood. In the workplace, males are more likely to view work as a competitive situation where there are winners and losers. Women are less likely to view work through the lens of being a competition.

These differences are slowly changing as more girls participate in team sports and gender expectations are less rigid. However, change is slow and we still place different expectations on males than we do on females.

While there are some noted differences in leadership style between the genders, it's this kind of intense focus on the differences that can serve to keep female leaders firmly below the glass ceiling.

Similarities Between Genders in Leadership
There are many more similarities between genders when it comes to how they lead than there are differences. So, let's take a look at how leaders are similar regardless of gender.

In many cases, it's the organizational culture that drives leadership behaviors more than gender. In a collaborative, non-hierarchical organization that emphasizes employee development, leaders are more likely to adopt transformational leadership behaviors. In a hierarchical, production-driven environment, behaviors consistent with transactional leadership will be adopted. Hiring managers look for leadership styles that fit with corporate culture, and so leaders that display a style congruent with the organization will stand a better chance of being hired.

In the Pew research, on the whole, the responses indicated that respondents didn't view many key leadership traits as significantly different for females or males. Competent leadership requires a blend of many different skills and competencies. Often, the specific competencies that a leader is strong in, are related to the context of the organization and are less dependent on gender.

One problem with perceived differences in leadership styles is that the terms used are subjective. People expect women to be more compassionate than men, and men to be more logical than women. This expectation can lead to them rating leaders differently based on gender expectations rather than reality. This can happen unconsciously, and so is potentially reflected in studies even when the questions are not overtly gender-specific.

Effective leadership requires several key competencies, none of which are exclusive to either gender. These competencies are skills that can be learned and developed by anybody regardless of gender.

Then there's the fact that the vast number of obvious and subtle differences between individual leaders goes way beyond gender differences. There are many compassionate and collaborative male leaders, just as there are many authoritarian and competitive female leaders.

Here's a list of the key traits that are commonly accepted as required for any individual to be an effective leader:

- Honesty and integrity
- Confidence
- Inspiring and motivating others
- Commitment and passion
- Good communication
- Decision making
- Problem-solving
- Delegation
- Innovation
- Empathy

As we've seen, women have the edge on some of these, but

none are exclusively female traits. Plenty of men are empathetic, and many women are very decisive. Being an effective leader is more about individually having the right blend of skills and capabilities to suit the job.

But if inherent gender traits aren't the reason that fewer women are in leadership positions, what's causing the disparity? One theory is that women simply don't want the responsibility of a high-level leadership position.

Do Enough Women Want To Be Leaders?

In 2003, an influential article was published in The New York Times. Journalist Lisa Belkin investigated why a growing number of successful women were 'opting out' of the corporate ladder, choosing to stay at home and raise their children instead.

The women featured had been afforded opportunities that women only twenty's five years earlier could only have dreamed of. They had Ivy League educations, prestigious law degrees and had gone on to gain prestigious positions in various organizations. The barriers to top-level leadership were coming down, and these women had the credentials to seize a piece of this power.

So why were they opting out of corporate life in high numbers? In the article, a theory was quoted that these women never broke through the glass ceiling because they were stopped by the 'maternal wall.' Those who didn't leave the world of work entirely were scaling down, reducing their hours and were not chasing higher positions in their organizations.

In the article, it noted that Fortune magazine had found that of the 108 women who had appeared on its list of the top 50 most powerful women, over 20 had since decided to leave their high-powered roles.

Why don't women rule the world? The article asks. Because they don't want to is the answer given.

Fast forward to the present day, and the idea of the opt-out revolution has come under a lot of scrutiny. In follow-up articles, many of the women had chosen to re-enter the world of work. They often took lower roles than those they'd occupied before, but many of them expressed some level of regret at giving up their ambition.

In 2013, a follow-up article was printed in the New York Times titled, *'The Opt-Out Generation Wants Back In.'* In the article, Judith Warner explored how the women featured in the original article and surrounding publicity now held different attitudes towards their decision to opt-out. In some cases, the women had since divorced and were left without the financial cushion of their husband's income that they'd relied upon to have the choice of opting out. For others, they felt that their identity and how their husbands viewed them had changed since opting out – and not for the better.

Another criticism leveled at the article has been that it focused on a very specific group of women. Predominantly white, middle class and privileged in terms of education, they were also married to affluent husbands and had the financial ability to choose to opt-out. For the majority of the female workforce 'opting out' has never really been a viable option.

So, is there an element of truth in the idea that women opt

themselves out of leadership roles once they marry and/or start a family?

The answer is complex. Yes, it's based on some truth. Women do often feel that they need to choose between career and family. There are still lingering societal pressures that make women feel like they are somehow failing their children if they aren't devoting their whole life to their upbringing. Combined with the fact that workplaces are generally more hostile places for working mothers, it feels easier for many women to either leave the workplace entirely or to accept that they will have to be content with lesser roles more 'suitable' for a working mother.

While more and more organizations have started to implement more family-friendly policies, it's still the case that flexibility simply isn't available in most workplaces. To 'get ahead' workers feel they need to work extra hours and spend as much time as possible in the office. Leaving early to spend time with their families or to take care of childcare responsibilities is often frowned upon in a lot of workplace cultures.

Requiring a degree of flexibility because of family responsibilities can be seen as being unreliable, and hiring managers can be put off by a woman who has children. Despite laws being put in place to discourage discrimination, it's easy for hiring managers to cite other reasons for rejection.

What this means is that while women might say they choose to stay home, the reality is that not all of them are making the choice freely. Often, giving up their ambitions is the only 'choice' they have.

Does Either Gender Really Make A More Effective Leader?

We've seen that in many competencies, women are considered more effective than men. The competencies where they are highest rated are those most commonly associated with transformational leadership. As leadership theory has evolved, transformational leadership is becoming the preferred style of leadership across most industries. Because of this, women do have a slight natural advantage.

Men, however also have natural characteristics that can lend themselves to a more transformational style. And like any other skill, these competencies can be learned.

The context of leadership is also relevant to how effective any individual leadership style is. The military, for example, lends itself to a more autocratic style. And the most effective leaders adapt their style for changing circumstances. While the inclusive nature of transformational leadership is an asset in many situations, a leader who won't make any decisions without consensus agreement is likely to lose trust and respect quite quickly. For urgent decisions that don't have a wide impact, a more autocratic decision-making process is much more effective.

The best leaders are those that understand the need for flexibility in leadership style regardless of gender or personal characteristics.

There's evidence to suggest that a more female-oriented style of leadership that takes a more mentoring and coaching style is best received in a more female-dominated environment. In a more male-dominated environment, a more autocratic and commanding style is better received.

In most modern organizations, a transformational leadership style is most effective. Large, successful businesses like Google and Apple are concentrating on removing rigidly hierarchical structures to promote creativity and problem-solving. The transformational, motivational style that emphasizes employee development and mentoring works very well in organizations like this.

In more hierarchical organizations like the military, this approach is less suitable. With clear and distinct boundaries and responsibilities between the different levels of leadership, a more autocratic approach ensures everyone understands their role. And when mistakes can have serious and far-reaching consequences, a transactional approach that rewards compliance and disciplines rule-breakers can be necessary.

Despite the already noted differences in male and female leadership styles, both men and women make effective leaders. The differences are apparent in various studies, but the percentages are small. The context of the leadership environment also has a large part to play.

It's also prudent to note that regardless of the study trends, psychologists have cautioned against concluding that either gender has a specific, natural management style. The research only demonstrates averages, and there is wild variance among individuals. It's also possible that women, having seen that adopting masculine behaviors has the undesired effect of making them unpopular, have consciously adapted towards more traditionally feminine traits.

Although the Fortune 500 is low on female CEOs, according to the Bureau of Labor Statistics, when you look at US organizations overall, nearly 25% of chief executives are women. On the surface, this looks like a big step forward, but these figures include small businesses with only a handful of employees.

Issues like the so-called Opt-Out Revolution are just the tip of the iceberg when it comes to reasons why there are significantly fewer female leaders. In Chapter Three, we'll investigate the second generation issues that could be holding women back from reaching their full leadership potential.

Chapter 3 – The Complicated 2nd Generation Gender Issues

"Women are not born, they are made."
Simone de Beauvoir, French writer, intellectual, existentialist philosopher, political activist, feminist and social theorist.

Gender Bias Issues

First-generation gender issues are the kind of issues we've briefly looked at so far. Open discrimination and exclusion from leadership or other positions were issues that our grandmothers and great-grandmothers often had to face. They were difficult to battle because they were deep-rooted, and society needed to change the way it viewed women in order to make a change. Overall, those big public battles have been won today.

There are federal laws in place protecting women from workplace discrimination. There are more women leaders than ever before, and society is constantly shifting towards a more positive view of women in high-powered roles.

Second-generation gender issues are less obvious and are more difficult to battle because so many people don't believe they exist or don't see them because of their subtlety. Many, but not all are workplace issues linked to policies created with male mindset or values. These are not intentional, and often seem to be completely non-sexist. However, they provide invisible barriers that prevent more women from rising through organizations to leadership roles.

In fact, second-generation issues are so subtle; many

women deny that they even exist. Yet research and studies have shown that they do, and they create very real barriers to women's success. For women experiencing these barriers, it can be very frustrating to be up against an almost invisible wall between you and workplace success.

So, what exactly are these barriers? How can you identify them? And how do you deal with them? In this chapter, we'll explore some of the most common second-generation issues in more detail.

Family and The Workplace

While men are contributing more to family responsibilities like childcare and housework than ever before, the simple fact is that women are usually still expected to be the main caregiver in the family.

When women choose to start a family, they are often diverting or delaying their career prospects, knowingly or not. Even with flexible working, family-friendly employer policies and a supportive husband, having children has a very real impact on women's careers.

Workplaces are usually not designed to support workers who may need flexibility in terms of hours and location. Many women are left with no alternative but to work part-time hours, which are usually lower-paid roles. Even if a woman manages to fulfill contracted hours in a full-time position, they are often barred from promotion by other invisible barriers.

Workplaces value employees who work longer hours, as it's seen to demonstrate commitment and ambition. Yet fulfilling contractual hours while also fulfilling caring duties and maintaining high-performance levels should also demonstrate the same thing. Unfortunately, as a society, we do not tend to see it this way or place value on such things.

Sometimes promotions may need extensive travel that would not be possible for a person who has family commitments. These requirements put women at a distinct disadvantage. Add this to the fact that if they have an ambitious spouse or partner, he will usually work long hours and do the traveling required – leaving the woman to pick up any additional family responsibilities. The idea that the woman would work the longer hours while the man makes career sacrifices more often than not isn't on the table for discussion.

What this means is that women 'choose' roles that are more flexible but have fewer, if any, opportunities for promotion.

If questioned about this, the usual response from hiring managers is 'but that's just what's needed for the job – regular travel, long hours, attending meetings.' Yet now, more than ever before, most things are possible to accomplish remotely. Live video calling and streaming mean that you can attend a meeting without setting foot in a meeting room and still get the benefits of face-to-face interaction with clients and colleagues.

There's another, insidious barrier affecting even women who choose not to have children – or find that they are not able to have children. Employers tend to discriminate against women who are of childbearing age, because of the expectation that at some point, the woman will have children. So where male colleagues are reaching the prime of their career, gaining promotions or successfully being hired by bigger and better organizations, women are struggling to be considered seriously because they pose the 'risk' to employers that they might have a child.

The impact of childcare responsibilities on women's careers is well-studied and accepted by most people. However, there's a hidden caring issue that impacts women more than men: taking care of elderly relatives.

When a parent or an in-law becomes unable to take care of themselves or needs extra support, it's usually the women of the family that provide that support. All too often, this happens just as the woman's childcare responsibilities are finished and her children are finally adults or older teenagers. As a result, many women who dreamed of picking up their careers once the children had grown up are faced with yet another dilemma: be there for someone they love that needs them, or put their career first. Understandably, it's their career that usually suffers.

While federal legislation does exist that provides some level of protection for pregnant women, the level of protection for women with childcare responsibilities varies by state. And there is nothing in place to protect people who care for elderly or disabled relatives.

Regardless of the reason behind women's roles as default caregivers, these extra responsibilities place a burden on their careers. Workplaces that don't have appropriately family-friendly policies can cause female employees, who have caregiving responsibilities, a lot of stress as they try to juggle the needs of their employer with the needs of their family. In this kind of environment, women with caregiving responsibilities can be viewed as less committed or less ambitious than their male counterparts, regardless of the quality of the work they produce. This, in turn, makes them less likely to be considered for senior roles.

Unconscious Gender Bias and How To Get Around It

On the whole, gender discrimination is something that most of us, even as women, can be unaware of. Part of the reason for that is our own unconscious bias. This bias is unconscious but strongly influences us when it comes to making decisions.

Research into cognitive bias has shown that we make conclusions about people very quickly, and most of our conclusions are based on our pre-programmed biases. Evidence of this can be found in the recruitment process, where both men and women have been shown to discriminate against female candidates for jobs or promotions without even realizing that they were doing it.

One such example in 1995 looked at a group of Swedish scientists. Researchers studied scientist's response to a selection of applications for research fellowships. Overwhelmingly, the scientists perceived women with the same number and level of accomplishment in the form of published scientific papers to be less competent than men with the same level of publications.

A simple change to anonymizing the applications by removing names removed the issue, and the candidates were then judged equally.

The unconscious nature of this bias makes it especially uncomfortable to address. People will vehemently deny that their behavior is biased because it isn't a conscious decision. Because of this, it can be uncomfortable to address. It can also lead to women silently suffer from the invisible barriers that can make them feel disconnected from their male colleagues and excluded from better roles and higher salaries.

So where does this unconscious bias come from?

It starts from very early childhood where we learn what activities, toys, and items are suitable for boys, and which are suitable for girls. Most children from age three or even earlier can apply a 'gender' to everyday items like dolls, make-up, and footballs.

So where do they learn this?

Everywhere. Television shows, books, adults, and other children are all constantly reinforcing gender rules and labels. Girls can wear dresses, but boys can't. Girls are not 'forbidden' to play football but children will rarely see this happening, and instead, they will see mostly, if not only, boys playing football. Commercials will show girls playing with dolls, and boys playing with train sets.

At the same time, more subtle gender rules about behavior are being reinforced. Boys are noisy, but girls should be quiet.

Of course, there are exceptions. Children will also be exposed to adults and other children who don't conform to all these rules and stereotypes. There are commercials showing both genders playing with items like building blocks and toy kitchens. There are television shows that have characters acting against stereotypes. Yet these are still the exception to the rule, and overwhelmingly children are still learning that there are significant differences between the genders.

Preschool children will usually choose to play with children of the same sex, where boys engage in more aggressive play involving physical contact, girls engage in more cooperative play. In larger groups, when boys do play with girls they show less aggression and more cooperation – and vice-versa.

In some senses, this early observation that there are differences between genders is natural and to be expected. What's important to take away is that there are differences between the genders, but the similarities far outweigh the differences. And not every person fits the societal norms. In fact, the very existence of gender expectations can cause harm. Consider the statistical fact that more men commit suicide. One common theory for this is that men are discouraged from opening up because talking about feelings is a 'female' behavior.

You may think, what's the harm? Perhaps girls naturally want to play with dolls, boys want to play with building blocks. However, the most recent research disagrees. Scientists are now leaning more heavily towards the conclusion that many perceived differences between men and women are heavily influenced by nurture, not nature.

Additionally, when you look at the skills these toys build in children, dolls teach nurturing and empathy, building blocks teach problem-solving and creativity. Are we doing girls a disservice by discouraging them from choosing toys that society considers to be masculine? And are we doing boys a disservice by discouraging them from developing nurturing and empathy skills?

We soak up these gender biases because they surround us.

Even if you don't agree with them, they are there in your subconscious. By the time we're ready to enter the workplace, we're already primed to consider men better leaders and women better secretaries – whether we realize it or not.

Linguistic Issues

Robin Lakoff investigated the idea of gender discrimination through language, and her findings were interesting. Lakoff concluded that men and women have different ways of expressing themselves through speech that add to the gender stereotypes that we see around us. In her book, *Language and Women's Place,* she suggested that one of the reasons women are perceived as weaker and less authoritative than men is down to the language they use.

She identified some linguistic behaviors that were more common among women than men, and that would add to this perception.

Women used exaggerated intonation that explicitly displays emotions like excitement, anger, and uncertainty. While men do use intonation, they were less likely to use it as often, or as exaggeratedly. By speaking in this way, others perceive women as more emotional – equaling a possible negative quality in the workplace.

Women also tended to seek approval for actions by tagging questions onto the end of requests or statements. Rather than directly stating, for example, 'I'm going out for lunch', women were more likely to say something like, 'I'm going out for lunch if that's ok?'

Another example is that women used a lot more hedging words. These are words and phrases like 'maybe' and 'just' that can indicate uncertainty or a lack of confidence in what you are saying. For example, whereas a man might say, 'I wanted to ask you a question," women are more likely to say, "I just wanted to ask you a question.'

Women are generally less direct in their speech, and more likely to give subtle (or not subtle) hints and cues that they want the listener to pick up on. They might say, 'It's a little hot in here', rather than, 'can you open a window?'

Women are more descriptive and use far more adjectives like 'lovely' and 'adorable.'

Women apologize more frequently and often apologize for the simple act of speaking or moving. Like this example – "I'm sorry, but I don't agree,"

Most of these examples illustrate how gender stereotypes displayed in language choices tell us that women should be polite, quiet, and unassertive. Women are less direct because they lack the innate feeling of authority to give instructions.

These are, of course, generalizations and women are perfectly capable of giving instructions, speaking directly, and keeping an unemotional tone. All of which are essential skills in leadership for specific situations. However, women show a distinct preference overall for speaking in a particular way that can unconsciously undermine their authority.

In-Group Favoritism
All humans have a natural preference for other people that are most like us. We prefer others who have a similar appearance to ourselves, and who have similar life

experiences and backgrounds. All friendships are formed based on some kind of common ground. We're naturally attracted to qualities in others that we see in ourselves.

It's an evolutionary bias, leftover from the days that humans lived in small tribes and outside tribes were a real potential threat. It's controlled by the more primitive part of our brain, and it's another unconscious bias that's fueled more by nature than by nurture.

Unfortunately, the implications are that we are more likely to hire and promote people who look, think, and behave as we do. When most leaders are still men, that unconscious bias serves to keep women out of leadership positions.

However, we've already shown that often even women will also favor a male candidate over a female one because of the unconscious gender biases that we all inherently carry. So why doesn't in-group favoritism win out in those situations?

In-group favoritism is a complicated bias. When we lived in small tribes, those tribes were naturally mixed gender. How we perceived 'otherness' wasn't limited to gender alone back then, and so it isn't only driven by gender today. Any time you identify yourself as in 'a group' you naturally begin to display biased behaviors where you favor people from that group.

The 'group' can be a literal group – classmates or a group of colleagues on a project. Or it can be a perceived group – people with similar hobbies, or even just people who wear the same brand of sneakers as you do. When faced with a choice, depending on which group you identify most strongly with, that bias will win out. So if a female hiring a manager identifies herself as in a group with her peers –

who happen to be mostly male, it can reduce or remove the in-group bias that might make her prefer the female candidate.

There's also the fact that in-group bias is much less pronounced when one group considers itself inferior to the other. The more strongly people identify with their group, and the more positive they feel about being part of that group, the more likely they are to display this type of bias. For groups who consider themselves superior, the in-group bias is strengthened.

As we've already seen, when it comes to leadership and the workplace, men are considered the superior group, even if this is an unconscious consideration. Which places women as the inferior group. Therefore, women in hiring positions are even less likely to display in-group favoritism based on their own gender.

In-group favoritism isn't a complete blocker to women's progression, and it isn't the only one – but that's partly the point. Combined with the other second-generation issues outlined in this chapter, it combines to make a perfect storm that keeps women behind invisible social and workplace barriers.

Exclusion From Professional Networks
A lot of job and promotion opportunities are linked to people's networks. As the adage goes, it's not what you know but who you know.

To start, the way men and women successfully network is different.

Men tend to have a very wide network but only a few close

connections. Whereas, a study found that female leaders with close ties to two or three other female leaders were more successful and benefited more from a smaller, closer network compared to their female counterparts who used a more male-dominated style of networking. Yet, the men who are part of the male-dominated networks are still much more successful than those more successful women in the study due to the better opportunities afforded by male networks.

And it's the exclusion from male-dominated networks that still very much hurt women's careers. Often women are unable to even join the networks and without access, some of the best jobs will always be just out of reach. Those jobs will be allocated without women even being considered for the roles. Even if we did somehow manage to get in, we still wouldn't get the same benefits as the males in the same network.

Another issue is that some male networking and business-related conversations often take place in venues that are inherently unwelcoming for women. Places like gentleman's clubs, golf courses or even more astounding, strip clubs, can be common places for males to meet male business clients or to discuss business with other men. These are intrinsically masculine places, which often make women feel uncomfortable, much less wish to conduct business negotiations or networking in these venues.

While women are not always explicitly excluded from entering these places, and indeed some women may particularly enjoy a round of golf, even there they are often segregated or differentiated in some way from the men – many clubs insist on different tees!

This is particularly common in industries like business to

business sales. It's often expected that a male client will be entertained in a venue like this. Even when women want to attend these venues with male colleagues, they are usually prevented from attending wherever possible.

Regardless of your moral stance on places like strip clubs, it's a reasonable assumption that organizations that allow and encourage business deals to be negotiated in them are openly discriminating against women.

Even where obvious exclusion due to venue choice isn't happening, women are still excluded both inside and outside of the workplace from men's social networks that offer those men a lot of valuable professional development opportunities.

Self-discrimination
We've touched on this several times in this chapter but it isn't only men that discriminate against women in the workplace. A number of the second generation issues are the result of masculine styles dominating businesses and organizations. As a result, those styles and expectations are being passed down and being held by lots of women too.

Some of the discrimination is from women who are naturally more masculine in their leadership style and have managed to reach a leadership position. Particularly in male-dominated industries, it's likely that they perceive themselves as part of the 'leadership' group of the industry and adopt the prevailing beliefs of that group-in-group favoritism in action. They are especially difficult to sway from their beliefs because if they managed to do it – why can't any woman intelligent and savvy enough follow in their footsteps?

Of course, not all female leaders hold this viewpoint, and plenty are true champions of gender equality but because of the unintentional nature of these particular biases, many women uphold them without even realizing it; as do many men.

Even more insidious is when women self-discriminate. You might question if that's even possible but human behavior is a complicated beast, and it's perfectly possible to sabotage your leadership career unconsciously.

Much of this is closely linked with mindset. It's becoming more and more recognized that the right mindset is the key to success but women in particular struggle with having the right mindset to set themselves up for that success.

Your mindset is made up of numerous internalized beliefs. Your concept of gender and gender rules and stereotypes are only part of your mindset. Your beliefs about money, power, leadership, and work that you've picked up both consciously and unconsciously over your lifetime all play into these beliefs.

The core problem of having a self-limiting mindset is that you naturally self-sabotage to validate your beliefs. People who want to earn a lot of money but have negative limiting beliefs about money, such as that rich people get richer and poor people stay poor, have a harder time motivating themselves to take the necessary action towards that goal.

Other people might believe that money only happens with hard work – the 60 hours plus work weeks and surviving on five hours of sleep a night kind of hard work. While hard work does usually pay off, that kind of working pattern will see most people fail from stress and exhaustion before they have a chance to reach their goals.

Women who hold limiting beliefs about their ability to lead – which may or may not be linked to their assumptions about gender – will always struggle to make progress.

A growth mindset is the most productive mindset, and it's also linked with a transformational leadership style – which we've already noted is the style most likely to lead to success.

A lot of deep-rooted self-limiting beliefs that hold women back in the workplace are linked to gender. Women might feel uncomfortable asking for a pay rise, and so find that they are not awarded anything because their manager has prioritized the department budget on those who did ask.

Women are taught that they shouldn't be too loud, shouldn't impose on others, shouldn't be pushy, shouldn't be greedy. While there are undoubtedly men that are brought up with the same beliefs, these particular limiting beliefs are almost always relevant to women.

These limiting beliefs can lead women to behave in the way they think they should, rather than how they want to behave. So they may give up work to raise a family when what they really wanted was to build a career alongside being a mother. Or they may not put themselves forward for promotions unless strongly encouraged, because they don't want to seem 'full of themselves.'

"I would venture to guess that Anon, who wrote so many poems without signing them, was often a woman."
Virginia Woolf, English writer.

Although plenty of women deny the existence of these second-generation issues, they are affecting the working lives of women in the Western world and beyond every day. Let's take a look at an example of a female professional who doesn't believe that she has experienced gender discrimination of any kind.

Real Life Case Study – Heather

Heather is a junior partner in a corporate law firm. As a lawyer, she's aware of gender and other forms of discrimination but firmly believes that she has not personally experienced gender discrimination. Heather graduated from an Ivy League law school. Her recollection of studying law there was that there were no differences in the treatment between the male and female students.

Heather chose corporate law, as this was the route she was encouraged down by her female careers advisor. She had considered litigation but her tutors and adviser felt that her skills matched better with corporate law. In fact, Heather can only remember one female student out the eighteen in her class opting to enter the litigation field.

Heather made junior partner after two years but she hasn't progressed since then. She points out that the only person to have progressed in that timeframe is her colleague Ben, and Heather admits he works longer hours than she does. Heather feels this isn't discriminatory because Heather is still unmarried and has no children – so her choice to work less than Ben is just evidence that he's more driven than she is.

In this case study, Heather denies that she's been subjected to discrimination of any kind. Yet between the lines of her story, there is evidence of unconscious biases. For example, women are often shepherded into particular educational/career choices.

When Heather's tutors encouraged her towards corporate law, chances are that they were encouraging all of the female students to go down that route. Why? Because of the unconscious gender bias that tells us women are not 'suitable' for litigation because they are too emotional or too 'soft' for trials. Society tells us that men are better at handling the pressure of litigation.

Undoubtedly, her tutor felt it was honest and genuine advice, and that it reflected her strengths based on assignment scores. Yet would her assignment scores have been the same if papers were marked anonymously?

Heather's lack of progression and her reasoning behind her male colleague deserving promotion more is also common. Heather feels that if she'd have worked longer hours, she might have been promoted. Yet she chose not to, and her colleague was promoted. Unfortunately, the acceptance of this kind of culture is still intrinsically detrimental to women. What if Heather does have children? Why are longer hours a sign of a better candidate? Surely performance is a better indicator of the right candidate?

Heather is optimistic about her chances for progression in the future. She points to the fact that there are women in two of the twelve senior leadership positions in the firm, whereas just ten years ago there were none. Surely, that's progress?

It's entirely possible that Heather will achieve her career ambitions. Many women can and do thrive in their careers – but when they do, it's against the invisible odds. The lack of women in high-level positions isn't a symptom of women's lack of ambition. It's second-generation gender issues.

Second generation issues can be difficult to spot, and it's even harder to get people to pay real attention to them. The gender discrimination cases we hear about are usually high-profile and blatantly obvious. Being dismissed for being pregnant would be obvious and easy grounds for a discrimination case.

Yet a recent UK survey highlighted that one in nine expectant mothers felt forced to leave their jobs. The majority of these were not dismissed or laid off. Instead, they believed they were being treated so unfairly that they had no choice but to leave. If that data was extrapolated, it could be assumed that over 50,000 pregnant women left the UK workforce because they felt forced and not because they chose to do so willingly.

In the next part of this book, we'll investigate how we define gender, look at gender stereotypes and identify what to expect if you choose to not conform to those stereotypes.

Chapter 4 – Gender, Equality and Getting Your Worth

"A gender-equal society would be one where the word 'gender' does not exist: where everyone can be themselves."
Gloria Steinem, American feminist, journalist, and social political activist.

Gender
We've talked a lot about gender so far but what does gender really mean? How did certain traits come to be defined as masculine or feminine? And how does the masculine vs. feminine debate impact leadership careers?

In this chapter, we'll explore and break down gender a little further and clarify some key concepts.

Masculine vs. Feminine
The words *'masculine'* and *'feminine'* usually conjure up certain images of men and women that fit stereotypes. But are these natural preconceptions, based on real biological and neurological differences between men and women? Or are they simply perceptions, constantly reinforced because of confirmation bias?

Of course, the concept of masculinity and femininity is related to certain behaviors rather than being biological constructs, although we tend to refer to physical features in this way too. Referring to a woman as masculine or a man as feminine is generally seen as an insult, a way to point them out as *'abnormal'* in the context of society as a whole.

To add to this, what's considered masculine and feminine varies between different cultures – indicating that what we perceive as masculine and feminine traits aren't biologically programmed but are instead influenced by what we see and hear around us. As such, they are generally learned attitudes and behaviors, a nurture issue rather than a nature one.

However, Neuroscientists have discovered that male and female brains do have some structural differences. For example, female brains have verbal centers on both the left and right hemispheres of the brain, whereas males only have a verbal center on the left hemisphere. Scientists believe that this is the reason that females tend to have more interest and skill in talking about feelings than males do.

Nonetheless, brains are still an individual quality, and these differences are very generalized. Male and female brains aren't like mass-produced items manufactured on a production line. While they are roughly uniform in size and function, there are numerous variables that can be different for every person regardless of their gender.

One recent study reported in *New Scientist* concluded that, *"averaged across many people, sex differences in brain structure do exist, but an individual brain is likely to be just that: individual, with a mix of features."* So there are neurological differences but these don't account for our perceived gender differences as much as we once thought.

What about hormones then, you may ask? Much is made of the effects that testosterone has on behaviors like competition and aggression but yet more recent research indicates that it isn't the magic potion that entirely explains masculine behaviors. While it is certainly linked to an increase in those behaviors, it isn't the singular driving force it has always been presumed to be.

Of course, our notions of competition and aggression are also cultural. Men and women can both be aggressive or competitive but the way they express that is often related to their culture's gender norms.

In the Western world, and many other developed countries, gender norms place men and women at polar opposites of the scale in terms of feelings, logic, practicality and nurturing. It's common in most cultures that women are perceived to be the ones in a partnership who will look after the home and children while a male partner goes to work.

Yet for all of society's insistence that men and women are very different, it's easy to overlook the fact that we're very similar. In psychology, there are five core personality traits: extraversion, openness, conscientiousness, neuroticism, and agreeableness. A study into how these traits varied between genders demonstrated that actually, there was less variance than expected. In fact, there was significant overlap between male and female participants.

Physically there are obvious differences in anatomy but psychologically we're much more alike than we are different.

Definition of Gender
The World Health Organization's definition of gender is: *"Gender refers to the socially constructed characteristics of women and men, such as norms, roles, and relationships of and between groups of women and men. It varies from society to society and can be changed."*

Gender is something of a loaded term. In the last few years, the concept of gender has been hotly debated. Challenges to our societal gender constructs have been more vocal. Many individuals feel that they don't 'fit' into the gender constructs that society has laid out for them and are pushing back against constructs that force them to choose if they are a 'man' or a 'woman.'

All too often, we confuse gender for sex. The sex of a person is generally determined by their genitalia and their genetic makeup – people with a 'Y' chromosome are considered male although there are rare genetic exceptions to even this 'rule'.

The gender of a person is a more abstract and fluid concept. It relates less to the biology of a person and more to the role of that person in society – how they identify and express themselves and how they are identified by others. It's possible to be born with both sets of genitalia, at which point in most countries the parents will choose which gender they assign to the child.

Gender Stereotypes and Roles
What is a gender stereotype? It's a preconception about attributes or characteristics of men and women; or about the roles that should be performed by women and men. They tend to be overly simplified, very generalized and very pervasive.

Gender roles are how society expects us to speak, behave, and look based on whether we're male or female. We've discussed at length so far what some of these expected roles and stereotypes are in the Western world. These stereotypes and roles are one reason why we still don't see many female engineers or airline pilots, or male childcare workers. If you ask a young child to draw a picture of a firefighter and a nurse, the chances are that the firefighter will be male and the nurse will be female.

But not only do these stereotypes vary across cultures, but they also vary over time and it's not always related to large social and political movements like women's rights. For example, you might be surprised to learn that as late as 1918, blue was considered a feminine color in the U.S. and pink was actually the more masculine color.

Even that pinnacle of stereotypical femininity, the high heel, was originally designed for men to wear while hunting on horseback. Over time, the style and design changed as women began wearing them, and as the high heel began to be associated more with femininity, men's shoes no longer incorporated such a high heel.

But are gender stereotypes really harmful? Many people will argue that these stereotypes exist precisely because they tend to be accurate, if generalized, reflections of how people of each gender dress, speak and behave.

The problem is that stereotypes are harmful when and if they place limits on both men and women's ability to make choices and pursue lives and careers that fit them as an individual. If a male is deterred from becoming a preschool teacher because it's a 'woman's' job then the stereotype is harmful. If a high school girl takes art instead of metalwork because 'metalwork is for boys' then it's harmful.

Negative stereotypes are the ones that are usually identified as harmful, such as women being over-emotional to the point of hysteria. Yet stereotypes that are presented as positives can still hold people back. Saying that women are caring and nurturing sounds like a good thing. Being caring and nurturing is a good thing, but it's not intrinsic to being a female.

However, that caring stereotype is one of the reasons that when an elderly relative needs care, it usually falls on the women in the family to pick it up. Men can and do take on caring responsibilities, but it's simply not expected that men will fulfill that role in the same way it is for women. This is all because of gender stereotypes.

For people in certain groups, like ethnic minorities or low economic status, the impact of existing gender stereotypes combined with other stereotypes for their groups can mean that they are even more heavily affected by the harmful effects of stereotyping.

On the surface, some stereotypes can seem harmless and even a little amusing, but recognizing all stereotypes for what they are and making an effort to look beyond them would result in a fairer and more comfortable world for most of us.

Questioning Femininity

"Always be a first-rate version of yourself instead of a second-rate version of somebody else."
Judy Garland, American singer, and actress.

We know that typically masculine traits are considered more desirable in leadership positions, and over the years women have received the advice to act more like men to get ahead. From wearing 1980's power suits with shoulder pads designed to give women a more masculine silhouette, to business coaches advising women to be me more masculine, the message has been 'if you can't beat them, join them'.

Studies have backed up this theory that masculine traits are more desirable in employees. In a 2017 experiment, researchers tested this theory by submitting graduate job applications across a wide range of sectors. Each application contained the same academic qualifications and experience but half emphasized masculine traits and hobbies like competitive sports and analytical thinking. The other half emphasized feminine traits and hobbies like embroidery and communication. The researchers found that the applications with masculine traits were 28% more likely to be invited to interview.

But what are the underlying issues and implications when women behave in a way that society deems masculine? Let's take a look at some examples of powerful women:

Hilary Clinton
The voting public usually expects all candidates to emulate strength and competence, which are two masculine traits. However, especially for women candidates, being too tough can lead to voters considering them to be insufficiently warm and engaging.

Over her career, Hilary developed a reputation for being 'too' ambitious. This is a criticism rarely aimed at men, whose ambition is often admired rather than criticized. In the media, everything from the shape of her mouth to the frequency with which she smiled was criticized.

Trump, as her political opponent frequently asserted that Hilary lacked the right 'temperament' or the stamina for the job of president. These accusations played heavily on the stereotypes of women as being overemotional, weak and fragile.

There's evidence that displaying masculine traits does cause female candidates to be less likable – but interestingly this effect is mostly confined to members of opposing parties. Their own parties are likely to view them more positively when they emphasize masculine traits.

Hilary's presidential campaign is a great example of in-group bias at play. Because of the context of the political arena, Democrats, on the whole, were great supporters of Hilary. Her party members viewed her as a strong and capable candidate. Republicans, however, found her less likable and not just because she was a Democrat. But because she was a woman behaving outside of expected gender norms. Had the Democrat candidate been a male, the chances are they would have been less strongly disliked or vilified by the opposition.

Margaret Thatcher

A remarkable woman, who was leading the UK at a time when female leaders were incredibly rare. She's often considered to have demonstrated many masculine traits, and famously had voice coaching in her early career to make her voice deeper – and therefore more authoritative.

Despite this, her political campaigning did quite often play to her feminine side. In one campaign she played to the housewife stereotype to appeal to female voters and potentially avoid the pitfalls of being labeled as 'too' masculine. In fact, she famously once said: *"perhaps it takes a housewife to see that Britain's national housekeeping is appalling."*

Although, she did not always conform to gender norms and was generally ambivalent about women's rights and feminism. Shortly after she gained leadership of the

Conservative Party, she was asked whether she saw it as a victory for women. She responded by saying, *"It is not a victory for women. It is a victory for someone in politics."*

Angela Merkel

In many ways, Angela Merkel has not overtly demonstrated masculine behaviors. If anything, she appears to have worked hard to present an image that is as gender-neutral as possible, while still identifying as a woman.

Still, she came under scrutiny early in her career for her frumpy exterior and sensible hair. She's usually seen wearing flat black shoes, pants and a suit jacket. It's difficult to imagine a male candidate coming under scrutiny for dressing in a sensible and tidy manner.

She's not entirely devoid of traits that could be considered masculine, however. She is considered ruthless when necessary, and particularly in her seizure of power in the wake of the scandal that saw her predecessor step down.

She also rarely, if ever displays any signs of emotion. It's her unruffled calm that makes her stand out when her male counterparts are allowing their emotions to get the better of them. This approach has worked very well. She's been leading Germany for well over a decade, and is generally well-liked and respected by voters and by her staff.

Golda Meir

Became Israel's first and only female prime minister in 1969. When questioned about how she felt becoming a female leader, she reacted in a similar way to Margaret Thatcher, responding, *"I don't know. I never was a man. This is who I am. Don't separate me as a woman. I am a person. I am a leader and that is how I should be seen."*

Despite her quote, David Ben-Gurion once famously said that Golda was, *"the only man in the cabinet,"* and Richard Nixon said of her, *"she acted like a man and wanted to be treated like a man."*

Again, like Margaret Thatcher, Golda Meir did not align herself with feminist groups and actively shunned them. The most likely reason for this is that she wanted to retain power in a political world that was still mostly dominated by men.

She was considered to be a strong personality with an indomitable will – generally masculine traits. However, Golda didn't hide her femininity and was not afraid to use it if she thought it would play to her advantage. She entertained foreign dignitaries in her kitchen, serving them home-cooked food while wearing an apron.

Despite initial popularity, the Yom Kippur war proved to be her downfall. Although under her leadership Israel won the war, the government was considered to have been unprepared and Golda was considered personally responsible for the deaths of thousands of Israeli men.

Several experts have posited that she was treated particularly harshly after the war because of her gender. Her decisiveness and actions were labeled 'arrogance' and people questioned how she could make military decisions having never been a general. Of course, as a woman at that time she was prohibited from serving in the army and so the underlying issue was at least partially one of gender, not specifically experience.

The examples of these women who have held some of the most powerful positions in the world show that it's possible to get ahead by embracing masculine traits but that there can be consequences. Arguably the most successful, Angela Merkel, adopts a more neutral approach rather than embodying either masculine or feminine traits.

Yet while women can get ahead by displaying masculine traits, there is a trade-off in terms of likeability. Society doesn't like it when people behave outside of their pre-conceived gender norms and so at best they have to find a way to justify it. At worst, they demonize it.

For the powerful women we've just discussed, people often justified their masculine traits by setting them apart from other women, as something 'other'. In some cases, even the leaders themselves avoided discussions of gender and steered conversations about their gender towards a more neutral approach.

However, none of them escaped scrutiny and sexist commentary. From the way they dressed to how they spoke, they have all at some point been scrutinized by the press and found wanting in some area of femininity. Interestingly, masculinity, whether it be lacking or overt, is something that you rarely have seen as being highlighted by the press in male leaders.

We know that masculine traits are more commonly associated with competence in the workplace, and an aura of competence is essential to be taken seriously as a leader. But we also know from studies that when people behave outside of gender expectations, then they instantly become less likable.

This puts women leaders in a double bind. They can behave in a masculine fashion and hopefully be seen as overall more competent, or they can be more widely liked and benefit from the advantages that brings. They usually can't have both. Even worse, there's no guarantee that they'll be successful regardless of which option they choose.

Overcoming Social Constructs and Constraints

In theory, women in the western world are not prohibited from entering any career field they choose. They can be engineers, leaders, judges, pharmacists, anything they want to be. However, women are still disproportionately represented in those roles. Why?

One reason is the pervasive gender stereotypes and roles that society place upon both genders. The only way to get beyond these is to slowly remove them, for both genders. The current problem is that one set of traits is seen as preferable to certain career choices, and we all feel invisible pressures to conform to our gender roles.

Then there's another aspect of the conversation. The possibility that perhaps women don't always want these traditionally masculine roles. Perhaps, goes the argument, many women gain more job satisfaction from traditionally 'feminine' roles, and will seek them out regardless. This is, indeed, possible. However, until we stop imposing gender norms, how can we quantify how many women choose these roles freely and how many choose these roles because they feel it's expected of them?

The key here is that there should always be a choice for anyone of any gender; a free choice unhindered by gender roles and expectations; a choice driven by the individual's wants, needs, and skills. The more we can steer ourselves and our organizations away from gender roles and expectations, the closer we will be to achieving equality. Yes, it's possible that given full equality, a majority of women will still choose roles in fields like education, arts and fewer will choose engineering or firefighting. But until the invisible barriers are lifted, we'll never know.

How and Why Should We Tackle These Issues?

We've spent a large part of the book so far looking at what issues women face, how these issues arose and how they impact women in the workplace as well as in society as a whole. This background information is necessary so that we all know what issues need to be overcome.

However, the fundamental question is what do we do about these issues? What can we do? What are the benefits of tackling these issues? In the next part of this book, we'll investigate how tackling these issues benefits everyone – not just women, and identify potential solutions to counter gender issues in the workplace.

Chapter 5 – Breaking Gender Barriers Down Fast

"The moral case for gender equality is obvious. It should not need any explanation."
Paul Polman, Business Leader.

Impact of Gender Barriers

Breaking down gender barriers doesn't just positively affect women, although, arguably it's women who stand to gain the most from a more equal society. However, gender stereotypes and roles can (and do!) have an adverse impact on men as well as women.

Let's consider for a moment the impact of gender stereotypes on men.

Men displaying traits associated with femininity can find themselves ridiculed, and men can feel just as much pressure to steer clear from careers traditionally associated with women. Men are often told that 'real' men don't cry. Crying is something that women do, a sign of their emotional instability and a sign of weakness. Yet in reality, crying is normal human behavior for both men and women. It's also a natural and powerful way to relieve emotional stress. Discouraging men from crying leaves them bottling up emotions that they're not sure how to express for fear of being seen as weak.

The flipside of men being the dominant gender in the workforce is that we tend to equate men's worth with their career. In particular, we associate their worth with their salary. High earning men are considered to be powerful. In contrast, women's worth tends to be tied to their looks or their nurturing abilities. Women are often left frustrated when their careers stall after childbirth. However, men feel immense pressure to be a suitable breadwinner in a household that's dropped from two incomes to one. It can also lead to men feeling embarrassed and emasculated if their female partner earns a higher income.

By breaking down gender barriers, we make strides towards a more just and equal society. Will it fix all of society's issues? No, but just like houses are built brick by brick, we need to lay the foundations of a just and equal society. Gender is one place to start.

Besides the altruistic reasons to promote more gender diverse workplaces, there are tangible business benefits to promoting diversity at work. Let's break down some of the key benefits that businesses can expect from becoming more gender diverse.

Benefits From Breaking Down Gender Stereotypes To Businesses And Organizations

"Women belong in all places where decisions are being made... It shouldn't be that women are the exception."
Ruth Bader Ginsburg, Associate justice of the U.S. Supreme Court.

Hire And Retain The Best People

Businesses exist for one reason – to make money and be successful. Even non-profits need to run their businesses effectively so that they can give more back to the groups that they are aiming to help.

To encourage better gender diversity, it's crucial that

businesses assess their hiring and promotion processes. These two processes are the biggest factor in promoting more diversity. Yet many companies still have hiring and promotion processes that put women at a distinct disadvantage. Unfortunately, this indirect discrimination against female candidates is also putting businesses at a distinct disadvantage.

Women make up half of the talent pool. Not only that, but according to the National Center for Education Statistics, they're the most qualified half. In the 2018-2019 academic year, women will earn over 57% of all awarded bachelor's degrees and over 51% of doctorates.

Women who do make it to the top of the corporate ladder tend to have more academic qualifications than their male colleagues. Yet, despite female graduates outnumbering men, they are less likely to be hired into entry-level jobs. At management-level jobs, this gap widens even further. Female candidates are much less likely to be hired into management level jobs. They are also much less likely to be promoted into them. Overall, only 38% of all management level positions are held by women.

If this doesn't change, the rate of growth in the number of women leaders is going to be painfully slow. When women are under-represented at every stage of the career ladder, it causes a knock-on effect of fewer women qualified to become C-suite leaders. Yet if companies start addressing these lower-level gaps now, we can close that gap much quicker.

More choice for women also means more candidate choices for businesses. In turn, this means that businesses can attract and retain the very best people for their organization. Creating career paths that are clearer, alongside working conditions less hostile to women, will allow women to be more motivated and driven to help the business succeed.

As we've discussed, there needs to be a focus on bottom-up hiring processes but there's also value in a focus on getting women into senior leadership roles. Once a business has recruited a good ratio of female leaders into its ranks, there's a trickle-down effect. Having more female senior leaders tends to lead to less gender discrimination in all recruitment processes in the business, including promotions.

<u>Simply Having A Diversity Policy Can Make You More Attractive To Potential Employees.</u> Millennials make up the largest segment of the workforce today. Research by UK consultancy PwC showed that over three-quarters of female millennials consider prospective employer's culture and their equality and diversity policies. In fact, 61% of women overall take into account the gender diversity of the leadership prospective employers when deciding where to work. By not having policies that promote diversity, you're potentially losing out on gaining some of the best talent.

It's important to note that a good hiring process doesn't mean favoring female candidates. It simply means that the process should encourage all candidates and allow the hiring manager to select the best person for the role. With that in mind, can any business really afford to discourage or ignore the most academically qualified half of the population when it comes to hiring?

Having a higher proportion of female leaders doesn't just lead to a better and more balanced recruitment process. It also leads to a lower staff turnover rate. Lower turnover is something that can save businesses a lot of money each year. When you're not spending large portions of your budget replacing staff who have left, you can concentrate on developing existing staff. This extra investment makes them more motivated and increases their loyalty and performance.

Higher Employee Engagement And Performance

It's a well-documented fact that employees who are more engaged with their organization are more productive, take fewer sick days and are better employees all around. As a result, most organizations place employee engagement high on their priority list.

Top business leaders understand that a high-performing workforce is essential for the growth of the business. The problem they face is how to achieve it. Regular surveys of employees give an indication of what can be improved but what is often overlooked is the importance of diverse workforces when it comes to engagement.

We've already covered how a lot of gender bias is unconscious and generally unintended – but that doesn't make it less harmful. When these biases go unnoticed, even by other women, it leaves us with a sense of unease. We know something isn't right, that we want something more from the organization's policies. Unfortunately, we aren't sure how to ask for it or even sometimes how to identify the problem. We don't feel fully engaged with the business but we don't know how to explain why.

Employee surveys have their place but results often show that people want more pay (not always possible across the board) and benefits. This results in employers introducing perks like free coffee, casual Fridays or employee competitions. These gimmicky solutions have a small place in engagement but they don't tend to drive real and sustainable engagement.

Studies have shown that a working environment that promotes diversity makes employees feel respected, engaged and involved with the business at a greater level. When this happens, employees are more productive and invested in their roles, and customers and clients receive better service.

Promote Creativity

Diversity also encourages collaboration, creativity and problem-solving – meaning you get more out of your employees. When diverse groups collaborate, the combination of unique perspectives leads to better ideas. The more diversity in a group, the more different perspectives can be considered. What's more, that feeling of inclusivity trickles down to your clients and customers making them more loyal to your brand.

In an interview with CNBC, Joe Carella, the assistant dean at the University of Arizona, Eller College of Management, confirmed that gender-diverse companies do become more creative. He said, *"We did our own analysis of Fortune 500 companies, and we found that companies that have women in top management roles experience what we call 'innovation intensity' and produce more patents — by an average of 20 percent more than teams with male leaders."*

There's lots of research demonstrating that diverse teams develop more innovative ideas. A diverse leadership team is more likely to promote an environment where ideas are shared, and creative ideas are considered. It's potentially down to the link between diversity and transformational leadership – which is also shown to encourage creative thinking.

However, to gain these benefits, your business needs to truly support and promote diversity. In order to contribute freely to discussions and generate innovative ideas and solutions, people need to feel safe and valued. If people don't feel safe to share their ideas or that their ideas are not valued by their peers and line management they will simply stop contributing.

It's not enough to just place more women in leadership positions. They need to feel safe and encouraged to contribute. When that happens, the boost to creativity can be remarkable.

Drive Business Profits and Performance
Having a gender-diverse business directly relates to having a more successful business. If business owners have been wondering why they should bother encouraging diversity then this is potentially the most compelling reason. If you're running a business, a healthier bottom line is always your key objective.

In fact, a McKinsey & Company report calculated that increasing gender diversity in the workplace could add $12 trillion to the global economy. Further research by McKinsey & Company demonstrated that businesses with a healthy balance of men and women are 15% more likely to outperform their competitors.

Clearly, the reasons for businesses to take gender diversity seriously are about more than just fairness and equality. Gender diversity isn't just a tick in the politically correct box: it's a competitive financial strategy.

Not convinced? A five-year study conducted by MSCI Inc into the performance of companies in the USA had some interesting insights. They found that businesses with a minimum of three women on the board had 45% higher earnings per share compared to those with none between

2011 and 2016.

A further Gallup study across two industries investigated over 800 business units. They discovered that gender-diverse business units generated an average of 14% more revenue and a 19% higher quarterly net profit than those with less diversity.

In yet another study, Harvard Kennedy School investigated employee gender in relation to sales and profits. They demonstrated that teams with an equal gender mix perform better than male-dominated teams in terms of sales and profits. They noted that sales and profits continued to increase proportionately in relation to the percentage of women, up to 50%. For teams with a higher proportion of women, there wasn't a decrease in performance compared to teams who were mostly male. However, they performed around the same level as the teams with an equal gender mix. What's especially interesting here is that the study looked at the performance of sales teams – which are typically male-dominated.

The relationship between high-performing companies and companies with a high percentage of female leaders is eye-opening. Research by the Peterson Institute for International Economics demonstrated that there is a correlation between higher profits and the number of women at the C-Suite. Companies with 30% or more leadership positions filled by women had at least 1% higher net profit margin when compared to companies without female leaders.

The amount of research demonstrating the relationship between a diverse leadership team and higher profit is staggering.

So why do the more diverse businesses perform better?

It's not necessarily true that women are better leaders but having more diversity at the decision-making level helps businesses perform better. In-group bias hurts business bottom-lines, and it's been demonstrated repeatedly that cultural diversity, as well as gender diversity, improves performance overall.

Without diversity at a senior level, a poor retention rate and disengaged employees could be the least of your issues. Shortly after the financial crisis, Sallie Krawcheck, co-founder and CEO of Ellevest and a former executive at Morgan Stanley and Citibank, blamed Wall Street's issue with 'groupthink' for contributing to the crisis. In an interview with CBS, she said: *"There was no doubt that had we had more diversity of thought, perspective, education, gender, color, the crisis would have been less severe."* She might have a point. In fact, after Iceland's banking crisis, the only bank left standing was headed by female leaders.

Attract Investors
In the same way that having a gender-diverse workforce and robust diversity policies can help you attract the best talent, they can also help you attract good investors. Several studies have highlighted that companies who adopt best practice policies, like a hiring process that encourages diversity, are seen as more attractive to investors. There's even research to suggest that when a business wins an award related to diversity, their stock prices increase.

However, there are caveats to this. An analysis of the research demonstrates that the industry context plays a large part in how much diversity affects investors. For industries that are traditionally male-dominated and less liberal culturally, the effect is diminished. For industries that are more liberal and aware of the benefits of promoting diversity, the effect is increased.

Having a gender-diverse workforce can positively impact how investors view the business and is highly unlikely to have any negative impact. As such, for businesses that haven't already done so, it makes excellent business sense to implement diversity policies as soon as possible.

The Vital Moves

Despite all the research showing the benefits, the academic performance of female students and the fact that it's the 21st century, many industries continue to be male-dominated. It's particularly obvious at the leadership level. Even now, 84% of engineers and architects are men, and computing isn't far behind.

The rise in numbers of women leaders is still slow, and even the companies that have gender-diversity policies and programs are not seeing the level of growth needed. But why?

In order to implement a successful gender diversity program, there needs to be a genuine desire to support women's leadership roles. All too often, businesses believe that hiring a token woman or two and paying lip service to gender diversity will 'solve the problem'. Unfortunately, this can create more problems than it solves.

As we've seen in earlier chapters, when women are placed into a male-dominated group, they too can begin to display in-group bias. Women who are the only females in a male-dominated leadership environment have a much harder time than when there is a true balance. They feel more pressure to fit in with male colleagues, and both they and the business they work for are less likely to experience the benefits associated with gender-diverse workplaces.

In contrast, when there are several female leaders at a senior level the real benefits of gender diversity begin to show. There's more collaboration, co-operation and a real embedding of gender diversity into the business culture.

Gender diversity is about more than meaningless quotas. In fact, a quota policy can breed distrust and resentment. Male colleagues can begin to feel that they are disadvantaged if there's an open quota to be filled. It can mean that even when women are promoted or hired on merit alone, they feel they have to work twice as hard to 'prove' that they deserve the role.

In contrast, when hiring and promotion policies are carefully reviewed to remove unconscious biases and barriers to female applicants, there will naturally be more successful female candidates. When it's clear that all roles are filled based on fair and robust criteria that don't disadvantage either gender, every successful candidate can begin their new role with the respect and support of all of their colleagues. It's important to promote the equality aspect – female-dominated departments can often benefit from more gender diversity as well.

Business leaders need to lead by example, promoting a culture of inclusion and open discussion. This way, all employees can raise concerns and have some input into how the business hires and promotes the best possible talent.

Real Life Case Study – David

David is the CEO of a large marketing consultancy. While his company continually made a profit, the level of profit had been stagnant year-on-year. Understandably, David wanted to drive the business to higher levels of success.

When his HR director presented him with a report citing research from Credit Suisse demonstrating an 18% return-on-investment premium for gender-diverse leadership teams, David knew he needed to pay attention.

Working closely with his HR team, David laid out his goals on achieving gender diversity in the business. His aim was to have a minimum of 30% of female leaders in the C-suite over the next five years. He also aimed to have all business departments with at least 40% of female employees.

To discover the best way to get the business there, David held a meeting with all of his current female employees to understand what barriers they faced, and how to remove them. His meeting uncovered that his female employees felt that the culture of long working hours was holding them back. Even if they produced the same amount and quality of work as employees who worked longer hours, his employees with caring responsibilities felt overlooked for recognition and promotion opportunities.

He also uncovered that there was a prevailing sense among female employees that the C-suite would be an unwelcoming environment for a female. When David asked why the employees felt the way, they mentioned that there was only one female leader out of nine board members.

David's first step was introducing a reward and recognition scheme that rewarded employees for high-quality work rather than excessive working hours. This immediate change addressed some of his employee's concerns about how the company valued employees with caring responsibilities.

His next step was to overhaul the hiring and promotion processes. Alongside his HR team, David reviewed the end to end process, from guidelines for placing an advertisement to how candidates were shortlisted. David took a radical approach. He suggested that all candidates who met the academic qualifications criteria were to be entered into a database. Via this database, the hiring managers could see the person's experience and qualification, but could not view the applicant's name, age, or gender. Based on this information, they could select the candidates for interview, who would be invited by the HR team.

By removing obvious identifiers of age or gender, David was removing a potential barrier for progressing female applicants. Each applicant could be judged on merit alone, making it more likely that a fair and diverse mix of candidates would be invited to interview.

Besides this radical change, they also removed any unnecessary insistence on inflexible working schedules. They also published their commitment to gender diversity on their corporate website and at the bottom of any literature relating to their hiring and promotions process.

The changes David implemented took over twelve months in total to embed and to begin to make a real difference. Over a 24 month period, the business saw a 10% increase of female employees at all levels and a 16% increase in the number of women promoted to a management level position. Over the same 24 month period, net profits rose by 4%, with projections for the following year being a total 6% increase.

So, we've covered why businesses should make an effort to break down gender barriers but how can everyone contribute to the cause? In the next chapter, we'll take a look at what individuals can do to promote gender equality in a positive way.

Chapter 6 – Your Own Choices

"We need women at all levels, including the top, to change the dynamic, reshape the conversation, to make sure women's voices are heard and heeded, not overlooked and ignored."
Sheryl Sandberg, American technology executive, author, and billionaire.

We've looked at the many ways that women are being held back in the workplace. While it's good to understand the background and why change needs to happen, what's even more important is to understand that you can also be a driver for change.

This book is all about empowering women to reach their potential in the workplace. It's about providing actionable advice for female leaders and aspiring leaders to implement. It's also to provide insights for hiring managers to improve gender diversity in their organizations.

So, with that in mind, let's take a look at what we can all do as individuals to improve the situation – for ourselves and for all women.

Achieving Confidence and Assertiveness

"It's not your job to like me, it's mine."
Byron Katie, American speaker and author.

We've discussed a lot of external factors preventing women from meeting their true potential in the workplace. Yet those barriers aren't the only thing holding women back. Sometimes, it's as much about mindset as it is about the environment that we work in.

Of course, the two things are linked. Your mindset is often heavily influenced by societal norms and what you perceive to be the truth of the way the world works. The barriers we've discussed so far influence your mindset without a doubt.

Luckily, your mindset is not a fixed thing. By recognizing issues as they arise and challenging your thinking and behavior, you can build a new more positive mindset that sets you up for success regardless of gender.

Change The Words You Use
Words hold a lot of power, and the words we use can shape other people's perceptions of us. With this in mind, it makes sense to be careful with the words we use about ourselves and others.

Women have a greater tendency to be self-deprecating, dismissive of praise, and overly polite or apologetic when asking for something or giving instruction. Perhaps it's because we believe that if we're straightforward, we might be labeled as 'a bitch' or overbearing. Yet men rarely make apologies simply for stating their opinion or asking a question, and this makes them appear more self-assured.

Women use a lot of filler words to soften their language. These are words and phrases like 'just', 'you see', and 'sort of'. When they're frequently used, they make the speaker sound unsure and unconfident.

Women are also more frequently apologetic. This can be a strength when used appropriately but when you're apologizing for having an opinion or daring to exist, then it is most certainly a weakness. By apologizing too much, and for the wrong things, you seem uncertain and weak.

Closely linked to being apologetic is the tendency to seek approval for ideas. Women are more likely to seek validation, whereas men are more likely to state their idea with the presumption that it will be challenged if it's not correct.

Women present their ideas in a manner that opens the idea up for criticism immediately. We invite and expect criticism rather than presenting the idea as though we expect it to be considered. The ability to accept criticism is an essential leadership skill but entering into every conversation expecting and inviting it is a different matter entirely.

<u>Be More Confident</u>
Self-doubt isn't an exclusively female trait but it is one that seems to plague many more women than men. On average, women gain more academic qualifications than men and earn higher grades, so why is that achievement not boosting women's confidence in their abilities?

We've previously looked at barriers in the workplace and society for women. In some cases, it's also this severe lack of confidence that's holding women back. Removing the barriers to promotion won't help if women won't put themselves forward for opportunities.

One study by Hewlett-Packard demonstrated that women would normally only apply for a position if they met 100% of the job requirements. For men, the threshold was 60%.

Women are more likely than men to believe they were 'lucky' to get a job offer or a promotion – even if their resume shows they are highly qualified for the role.

Women are also more likely to question their abilities and suffer from 'Imposter Syndrome'.

Sheryl Sandberg, Facebook's COO has been quoted as saying, *"There are still days I wake up feeling like a fraud, not sure I should be where I am."*

Women are less likely to ask for a pay rise or a promotion. Instead, they put all their effort into their work and hope to be noticed and rewarded for an excellent performance. In the meantime, their male colleagues are more likely to ask for what they want directly – and consequently more likely to get it. Even when women do negotiate salary increases, they set their sights approximately 30% lower than men do, which means even when they do ask, they generally receive less.

It's a proven fact that self-confidence and appearing confident are important factors leading to success. Confidence can be equal to competence when it comes to achieving career success. So, it's vital that women start to believe in themselves and their abilities.

One thing that holds women back from being more confident is the fear that they might be seen as arrogant if they have the same unshakeable self-confidence that a lot of male leaders seem to exude. However, confidence is very different from arrogance. Taking steps to be more assertive can help you come across as more confident – without appearing arrogant.

Be Assertive
Assertive behavior is a key leadership skill, regardless of gender. However, women often have a harder time displaying assertive traits because they tend to be perceived as 'male' traits. Women can sometimes shy away from

being assertive in case they are perceived as 'bossy' or 'aggressive'. However, a lot of assertive traits are quite 'female'.

Being assertive is very different from being bossy, arrogant, or aggressive, and it's something that all leaders should be aiming to develop. Assertive leaders express their thoughts and their feelings in a direct, honest, and appropriate way. Because of this, they often gain the trust and respect of their teams and their peers.

Assertive leaders are collaborative. They listen and respect the thoughts and feelings of others – a trait more often associated with women.

Assertion is closely linked to communication skills, something that women tend to be good at. Where women sometimes fall is in how clearly they communicate their own needs and goals. Adopting an assertive communication style when discussing promotion opportunities and pay rises can help you come across more confidently and authoritatively.

When assertive people discuss opportunities, they usually present clear and succinct evidence to back up why they should be considered for a promotion or pay increase. By calmly and clearly stating their case, they make it easy for their line manager to both understand what is being requested, and why they should consider it.

Assertive people tend to know their worth, and they accept that another person's opinion of them does not define them as a person. This might seem counter-intuitive to the idea that a good leader needs to have a certain 'image'. However, an assertive approach accepts that not everyone will like you or agree with you. Assertive leaders listen and take other's opinions on board. They might change their own opinion based on the argument of another person but they never back down out of fear or rejection because they know they are worth more than that.

Being assertive offers many benefits. By learning to be more assertive, you can effectively express your feelings in a way that others can understand. It allows you to be clear about what your needs are so that others can meet them.

It also helps you keep people from taking advantage of you, and ensures that your opinions are heard. Behaving assertively can help you gain the respect of others, and in turn, improve your confidence and self-esteem.

Need a quick way to become more assertive immediately? – Stand up!

A study from Washington University showed that simply standing up can make you automatically more assertive. They noted that when people stand up or move around more, they are also more creative and collaborative. According to another study by Stanford, a brief walk also boosted creativity, which is linked to assertion. To reap the benefits, try and move or stand more during the working day.

Ditch Perfectionism and Trying To 'Have It All'

"It is impossible to live without failing at something, unless you live so cautiously that you might as well not have lived at all – in which case, you fail by default."

J. K. Rowling, British novelist.

Perfectionism is something that plagues women. For some reason, women believe they need to be as perfect as possible. It's not uncommon for women to triple-check every report they send and beat themselves up mentally if they miss a typo. Many women will avoid putting forward an opinion in a meeting unless they're sure they understand the topic as well as an expert.

There's a damaging ideal that exists of the woman who 'has it all'. You know the one, the woman holding down a prestigious high-level management role. She has several perfectly well-adjusted children, a perfect home, holds regular dinner parties, and never has a hair out of place.

The thing is, she doesn't exist, and women need to stop trying to be her. Sure, there might be days or weeks when women can meet these exacting standards we set for ourselves but it's just not sustainable, or good for mental health, in the long term.

Am I telling you to stop trying to achieve big things at work and home? Not at all. It's important to understand the difference between aiming big and perfectionism.

This advice isn't to stop dreaming big, aiming high, and wanting to be the best you can be at everything. In fact, that's the point. Aim high, dream big. Be the best you can be.

If you're struggling and making compromises to hold down a career and a family, that's ok. You're not failing. By all means, look for solutions and improve your situation. But don't put yourself down because you're holding yourself to an impossible ideal and feel like you are 'failing' that ideal.

Social media makes this type of perfectionism even worse. Depending on who you have on your social media feeds, you might be overwhelmed with images of women who are 'perfect'. They seem to have perfect families, perfect make-up, perfect bodies. The problem is that it's easy to manipulate the image we present on social media. Just because somebody's life appears to be a certain way, doesn't make it that way in real life.

Stop comparing yourself, stop trying to uphold an unrealistic image of yourself. Aim high but accept that failure and setbacks are part of life for everybody. With an assertive, positive mindset you will begin to look at these as opportunities to learn and improve. Letting go of perfectionism allows you to take more action, get more done, and potentially make more progress in your career.

Create 'Me' Time To Grow And Nurture Yourself

It's important to take time out for self-development and self-care. What that looks like can be different for every individual but the key is to create the time, protect it, and use it in the best possible way.

It might be meditation; it might be time to reflect, plan, and set goals for yourself. It might be a spa day. It could be time to complete online courses or time to attend a night class. Whatever energizes you and helps you grow as a leader.

We live in a culture where hard work and long hours are seen as the ultimate keys to success. There's nothing wrong with hard work but working smarter and not needing to work excessive hours is a much better way. Unfortunately, our obsession with being productive and working long hours means we end up exhausted and burned out –

regardless of gender. And if you happen to have caring responsibilities like the majority of women, then getting everything done can seem overwhelming.

Taking time out to develop yourself or to practice self-care can seem like an indulgence you can't afford. In reality, it's a necessity you can't afford to ignore. When you're energized and well-rested, you can bring the best possible version of you to work. Investing time and effort in developing your knowledge and skills gives you the confidence boost to present the kind of self-assured persona that we already know contributes to success.

Stop putting yourself last on the list and secretly hoping someone will notice and give you a break. Give yourself a break and demonstrate that you value yourself. It won't be long before others pick up on the energy and start to recognize your value too.

Building Your Tribe

All the above are things you can do alone to develop the right mindset for success. The following suggestions are things you can do to get the support you need to succeed. These relate to building your authority as a female leader or entrepreneur and finding yourself a 'tribe' of like-minded women to support and encourage each other. We're keeping them in the 'what you can do alone' chapter because we're focusing on your specific part in joining and creating this tribe.

Embrace Your Femininity
We know that simply behaving like a man doesn't usually work for women in the workplace. While there are certain

lessons we can learn from the way men tend to do things; being more confident and less perfectionist, behaving in a way that feels unnatural will come across as untrue to others and might even make you unhappy.

For many reasons, women, in general, have a different perspective on life than men. This is a huge generalization but it holds true in many areas. Instead of seeing this a weakness, or focusing on negative differences, we can embrace the diversity of thought this brings, and use it to our advantage.

We already know that diverse workplaces are more creative, productive, and profitable – and it's all down to having a mix of perspectives and opinions to be considered. When management meetings and board meetings have a diverse range of people in them, the decisions made usually better reflect the needs of the end client or consumer.

So instead of agreeing with male colleagues for the sake of it or censoring your opinions because you're worried that they might be 'too' something – too emotional, too loud, too different, put your thoughts and opinions out there with confidence. If people don't agree that's fine but why not share what you have to offer and keep on doing it?

For example, when faced with handling a difficult member of staff, embrace your natural ability to empathize and listen. Use it to persuade the member of staff to change their behavior.

Not all women (or men) have the same innate traits, and that's absolutely as it should be. What I'm advocating here is that you embrace you. Allow yourself to express your opinions and handle situations in a way that makes the best use of your strengths – instead of trying to fit a mold made for somebody else.

Build A Network

Networks are essential for success but when women try to build a network in the same way as men, it doesn't give them the same success. So what's different about the way men and women network?

Men have broader networks, filled with casual relationships, whereas women tend to cultivate smaller networks with deeper relationships. Because men have wider networks, they can access more opportunities through that network. However, it's not all bad news for women.

The deeper relationships that women build can be very supportive, and when opportunities do arise, their network contacts are more likely to champion them for the role. Studies have shown that when women build networks that include other successful women, they achieve greater success than women who adopt a broader network in the style of male colleagues.

This doesn't mean you need a women-only network and that you should avoid networking with men. However, it does mean that you probably don't want to follow the same networking strategy as men. Ideally, you should seek to have as many successful and ambitious women in your network as possible.

Obviously, there are a lot fewer female leaders than there are male leaders, so alongside building your in-person network, taking advantage of online networks can give your career a boost.

Online networks like Girlboss gives you access to other

professionals, and with a female-heavy population, Girlboss is a great place to start. Despite the name, it's not a female-only network but it's the positive message of female empowerment attracts some of the best and brightest female talent.

Founded by Sophia Amoruso, a seriously successful serial entrepreneur, Girlboss aims to fill the gap that more traditional online networking sites like LinkedIn haven't managed to address. And alongside the networking aspect, there are also educational tools like podcasts and conferences aimed towards empowering more female leaders.

Networking, whether in-person or online, can be a very powerful career tool. It doesn't come naturally to everybody, and in-person networking can sometimes seem intimidating if you're not naturally self-assured.

One way to overcome this is to look at networking for what it is: building relationships. You can network at the coffee shop, the school gates, in the supermarket… Anywhere there are people you can speak to, you can network. Strike up a conversation wherever you're comfortable and find out about people. Some of the most interesting contacts can come out of the simple small talk struck up in unlikely networking places.

When you identify that someone might be a good addition to your network, hand them a business card, and schedule a follow-up meeting. The follow-up doesn't have to be formal, a casual conversation over coffee can be the perfect follow-up.

Networking events and groups are a better way to immediately connect with other professionals but beware that they can be intimidating at first. To take away some of the trepidation, prepare your 'elevator pitch' in advance and practice saying it out loud. That way, when you're inevitably asked, 'what do you do?', you'll be able to respond without nerves getting in the way.

Some cities even host female-only networking groups, which many women may find a more comfortable environment. Check for these being advertised on LinkedIn or other social media.

Look For An In-House Sponsor
Having a sponsor can give your career a real boost. It's important to note that a sponsor is different than a mentor. Mentors are excellent for advising you and guiding you in your career. A sponsor, however, is your own personal champion.

Mentors are also important to provide advice and support. Ideally, your mentor should be at the next step in their career compared to you. This way, they still understand the challenges you face at your current level, as well as being able to prepare you for the challenges the next level will bring.

You're not limited to just one mentor. You can have several but ideally with different experience and strengths so that you can learn from each of them differently. Lots of companies have a program to match you with a mentor but if your organization doesn't have one, it's worth seeking out a mentor on your own.

It's possible for someone to be both your mentor and your sponsor but the roles are very different. A sponsor doesn't always offer the same kind of support that a mentor does and vice versa.

Sponsors can help you bridge the gap from operation management to strategic management – something that many women can struggle with. A sponsor is always someone at least one management level above you. The idea is that they are championing you behind doors that are usually closed to you, like in board meetings.

A sponsor can put your name forward for big projects, promotions, and any opportunities that come up that might further your career. Because of this, your sponsor should be as senior as possible. Because they need to be able to get behind all of the organizational doors that are closed to you, the more senior and influential they are, the better.

Your sponsor doesn't have to be female. In fact, given the lack of females in high-level leadership roles, you may not be able to find a female sponsor within your organization. However, if you can find a female sponsor, then that's another great way to include successful females in your network.

Organizations don't usually offer programs to find a sponsor as they do with mentors, so it will be up to you to identify a build a relationship with a suitable sponsor.

Become A Subject Matter Expert And Thought Leader
We already know that women do better academically than men but then why are so many 'experts' in the press and on television men? That's not to say men can't be experts but it seems very disproportionate given that, statistically, men don't achieve higher grades academically.

Mostly, it stems from the self-confidence issue, coupled with the invisible barriers we've discussed in previous chapters. But it's time women stood up and claimed their expertise.

So, what is a subject matter expert? It's someone who knows more than most people about a topic. You don't have to know every single detail about the topic to be an expert but you do need to have a deep understanding of it.

Obviously, context matters. You can't enjoy reading articles and books on neuroscience and then set yourself up as an 'expert' in it without a formal education. Even if you do have excellent knowledge on the topic from self-study, academic expertise often requires academic qualifications and even potentially requires tenured experience.

If, however, you're the go-to person in your organization if someone wants to know about the tender process for procurement, then you're probably a subject matter expert. Identify a topic where your knowledge and experience exceeds the knowledge and experience of other individuals in your organization, and that's where you're potentially an expert.

Being an expert usually involves not just knowing about something but also having applied that knowledge in some way in the real world – ideally with some kind of proven results. Often, women do have the expertise, even including the academic qualifications to back that up – and yet don't claim that expertise.

If you know about a topic relevant to your company or industry, and you find people coming to you for help and advice – own it, build on it and celebrate it. You're a subject matter expert.

Once you're recognized as a subject matter expert on something, you can leverage your knowledge and expertise to become a thought leader. Thought leaders use their expertise to devise strategies and identify potential issues that can be avoided. For example, your expertise might be in marketing. You can be a thought leader by using your knowledge of up-and-coming marketing technology and trends to identify good areas for your organization to invest in – and avoid areas that you believe won't be as successful.

Depending on your subject, you could write an article on your area of expertise and maybe even pitch it to a big publication. Not a big writer? Appear as a guest on podcasts, attend business networking focus groups to talk about it. If it's limited to your particular organization, why not create a company Wiki on the topic or a training manual for others?

Find ways to leverage the knowledge you have, along with ways of building on that knowledge – and share it with the world, or at least your colleagues. You'll gain recognition and respect that are natural springboards into leadership.

Use Feedforward
Feedforward is a great feedback tool for all leaders but it can be put to particularly good use for female leaders looking to improve how others perceive them.

Asking for feedback can be a nerve-wrecking experience no matter your managerial level, and giving feedback to people more senior than you can also be nerve-wrecking. Feedforward can make it easier for both parties.

If you're not familiar with the concept, here's how feedforward works:
1. Choose a behavior that you want to change. It could be to contribute more often in meetings or to stop

using overly apologetic language.
2. Explain your goal to a colleague in a one-to-one setting.
3. Ask the person if they have two ideas on how you can achieve your goal, and listen attentively to their response. You are not allowed to challenge their response, simply listen. The only response you are allowed to give is 'thank you'.
4. Once you've done this, you repeat the same process with a different person.

So, why does it work better than more traditional methods of feedback? Marshall Goldsmith, the creator of the feedforward method, suggests that this method feels less uncomfortable, and therefore is easier to initiate. It also feels less intense, as you're not specifically asking people for their opinions on you, per se.

You're asking a general question on how you can reach a specific goal. Their advice is likely to take into account how they perceive you, so it's personal and specific advice. You receive the information you need without openly seeking criticism or having the information framed in a way that is likely to make anyone uncomfortable.

It's also a great way to focus on the future. Traditional feedback is, by nature, quite focused on your past behaviors. While you can learn a lot from your past behaviors, dwelling on what you did before is much less helpful than focusing on what you can do in the future.

Be Heard
If there's one thing every woman should at least try to do, it's to speak up. If you come across gender bias, call it out. You don't have to be confrontational about it. Handle it in a way that feels comfortable for you but don't let it slip by

unchecked.

Unfortunately, speaking up won't always help if you're not being heard. So how do you make sure that you're being heard?

Consider forming amplification groups with like-minded female colleagues. The concept of amplification emerged after a former female White House official confided to journalists that women in the White House had at times found it so difficult to be heard that they created amplification groups.

The purpose of amplification was for the women in the White House to literally 'amplify' other women's comments and ideas by repeating them and backing them. If a woman offered a comment or idea that was ignored in a meeting, another woman would repeat it, crediting the original woman who offered it. By doing this, it became very difficult for women's ideas to go unheard.

By forming amplification groups, and making use of all potential amplifiers, not only can women join together to call out gender-biased policies and practices, they can ensure that they are heard.

It's a cliché, but it's true. We need to become the change that we want to see. Applying these ideas to your own life can help you make personal progress towards becoming a great leader regardless of gender.

However, there's also a lot that women can do together. In the next chapter, we'll investigate some broad-based strategies that can help push change faster and further.

Chapter 7 – Broader Strategies For Everyday Use

"The women who have achieved success in the various fields of labour have won the victory for us, but unless we all follow up and press onward the advantage will be lost. Yesterday's successes will not do for today!"
Nellie McClung, Canadian author, social activist, suffragette, and politician.

The Case We Must Make

We've looked fairly closely at what individual women can do to address gender bias in the workplace, including building networks and joining together to form amplification groups. However, these strategies are very small scale.

These individual actions do make a difference. However, for real and effective change, it's going to take a combination of individual and collective actions, including broad-based strategies that businesses can implement.

Inclusivity Starts With The Hiring Process
It's probably stating the obvious that companies need to hire more women into senior roles, or roles that are likely to lead to senior positions in the future.

It makes sense to review hiring processes to ensure that they're as fair and robust as possible. Staff costs are usually one of the highest costs that any business bears and getting it wrong can be expensive.

Reviewing hiring processes to ensure that your company is hiring the best person for the role means successful candidates are more likely to stay with the business for longer. Your business gets better results and saves money on rehiring for the same role.

So what are some changes that you can implement to help eliminate gender bias from the hiring process?

Remove Identifying Details At Application
Consider removing identifying details from applications at the review stage. When the hiring managers can't see factors like names and ages, it's much harder for unconscious bias to creep in.

Your assessment and interview processes should be set up to support hiring managers to identify the best candidate for the role. All interview questions should be vetted to make sure there are no hidden gender biases.

Obviously, it's difficult to conceal gender at an interview. Interviewing managers should be trained in unconscious biases and experienced at hiring diverse people. Where the hiring manager lacks this experience, provide training and have them supported by an appropriate person who does have experience.

Your interviewers should be as diverse as possible so that in-group biases don't easily win out. Wherever possible:

Offer Equal Pay For Equal Work

"I may sometimes be willing to teach for nothing, but if paid at all, I shall never do a man's work for less than a man's pay."
Clara Barton, founder of the American Red Cross.

When establishing an appropriate starting salary, it's particularly important to make sure that you're not offering a lower rate to female candidates than an equally experienced male candidate. The starting salary should be commensurate with the role responsibilities. A candidate's previous salary history should not influence the salary you offer. Otherwise, you're potentially carrying over gender bias from other businesses into your own.

Your equal pay policy shouldn't end with new recruits. Existing gaps should be addressed, and salaries should be regularly reviewed to ensure that disparity hasn't been introduced over time as people receive performance-related pay rises and promotions.

Of course, the disparity in pay often first occurs when a woman decides to start a family. Creating more flexible working options for all employees including remote working, job shares, and consulting assignments will help you retain more women. It also prevents depreciation in salary because of a need to pause or step down in their career to accommodate family responsibilities.

It's important that all employees have the option for these benefits. While it can help to offer female employees more flexibility, if the same opportunities are not extended to male colleagues or colleagues without children, it can create hostility.

Design Roles Around People
Hire smart, capable people and design the role around them. What is often overlooked is that it's not enough to just change the hiring processes. You also need to change the roles you're hiring into. Trying to shoehorn women into roles that have been designed with men in mind – whether

consciously or not – isn't going to work.

The traditional hiring process is seldom questioned. Companies decide what they need, create a job role, and then hire for it. When the person in that role leaves or is promoted, they look for a replacement into the exact same role.

Even when businesses have enough foresight to review roles when an employee leaves or is promoted, they still define the role tightly before advertising and hiring.

There are a couple of things that make this traditional approach problematic. Firstly, there's a chance that the existing role holds some level of gender bias. If you're explicitly stating you need someone who is flexible around working longer hours, you're preventing people with caring responsibilities from applying.

There are obviously elements of the job role that will need to be clearly and strictly defined. If you're hiring for a Head of Sales, some managerial experience and sales experience will be necessary to perform the role. Keeping your non-negotiables in the job description is helpful but try not to include the 'nice to have' elements in the job role that you advertise. We've already seen that women will only apply if they meet 100% of the criteria. Having too many 'nice to haves' will cause many women to avoid applying even if they are completely qualified for the role.

For example, if your Head of Marketing left to work for a competitor, instead of dusting off their job description, making cursory changes and posting a job ad, you'd think about the actual outcomes you need from this role. Not the minutiae of the duties but the outcomes and the skills needed to achieve them.

By hiring the right person and then developing the role to leverage the person's strengths and talents, you'll get the best out of your new employee and open up a world of possibilities for the business.

Career Development Support

Hiring more women should be just the start of the process. Companies can do more to nurture women's careers by implementing programs for all employees designed to encourage more diversity in leadership roles.

By investing in hiring, mentoring, sponsorship, and career development, businesses can help ensure that women can attain and retain demanding positions. For businesses willing to commit to this, they will be laying the foundations for a serious competitive advantage in the long term.

Sponsorship

We discussed sponsorship earlier, from the point of view of a woman seeking out a sponsor to champion them. From the other side, women and people at a senior level can look out for suitable women to sponsor.

By implementing an official sponsorship program, you can identify your top talent and pair them with a sponsor to ensure that there is somebody at a high level championing them. By making the sponsorship official, it becomes a transparent process that can be evaluated to make sure it's promoting diversity as intended.

Mentorship

Lots of businesses already have mentorship programs but they are a great way to support and nurture employee development. They're particularly useful when beginning a new role, to help coach and support.

If you're a very small business, you can connect employees with mentors in similar roles outside of your business. Your local chamber of commerce may even be able to help.

Career Counseling

Career counseling involves making sure that everyone is aware of the career paths open to them. By having regular and open conversations with employees about their ambitions, and the skills and qualifications needed to progress to the next step, you can keep them motivated and engaged.

It also ensures that your talented but more introverted employees don't fall by the wayside simply because they don't aggressively seek out opportunity.

These conversations should be incorporated into regular performance reviews so that conversations about promotions and career progression are specifically linked to employee performance.

Reward Performance Fairly

Reward and recognition schemes can often favor men. Although it's usually an unconscious bias, it's a pervasive one. Examples of schemes that unfairly penalize or restrict women are:

- Only offering bonuses in male-dominated departments, like sales departments.
- Rewarding performance linked with working longer hours, like sheer volume rather than the quality of work. If volume is a key metric, any additional hours worked should be taken into consideration and a production rate per hour might be more appropriate.

- Schemes that reward length of service. Women are more likely to experience a break in employment because of their caring responsibilities.
- Bonuses offered without a clear and transparent framework. For example, a discretionary bonus given by managers without very clear criteria to assess employees against. Studies have shown that even when male and female employees achieve the same goals, the male employee's achievement is often viewed as more impressive.
- Schemes that penalize part-time workers, who are usually women.

Small Businesses Can Lead The Way

Small business owners may feel that the diversity issue isn't one that applies as heavily to them. Small businesses don't have as many employees, and for very small businesses who only employ a few employees, the small numbers can mean that it's almost impossible to achieve a % quota of female leaders.

However, diversity is about a lot more than quotas. For large businesses quotas can be one way that they can have an easy way to identify to measure how they're doing. In a small business, you don't need to do that but you still stand to gain a lot from having a diverse workforce.

Small businesses have a real opportunity to level the playing field. By their nature, smaller businesses are more agile and can make changes quickly without the bureaucratic red tape that plagues multi-national organizations.

Smaller businesses can quickly implement initiatives like creating partnerships with local schools to offer work experience programs to students. And, with a shorter chain of command, filtering cultural change down through the ranks and leading by example is also easier.

The challenges smaller businesses might face is that they may recruit and promote less often, meaning that any changes to their processes could take additional time to be reflected in their leadership team.

However, smaller businesses can lay the foundations for a diverse future by starting to implement changes now so that they can reap the rewards later.

Real Life Case Study – How IBM Encourages Gender Diversity

IBM takes diversity very seriously, with diversity initiatives that go way beyond gender diversity and include various minority groups. Let's take a look at some of their initiatives that focus on gender diversity.

Headed by a female CEO, you could argue that IBM has a head start but they recognize that encouraging diversity is an ongoing and necessary task. Having female leaders isn't 'the end' of a real diversity initiative.

Their diversity programs are particularly effective because they consider diversity as an essential part of their business success, alongside innovation. They embrace diversity as a key differentiator between themselves and their competition and leverage the creative advantage that creates.

IBM runs several programs to attract females to a career in

the IT industry. One of these programs is the Girls Schools' Outreach Program, which was established in 2008 by the UK Women's Leadership Council. The program connects girls aged 15-16 with mentors from IBM and provides work experience for over a hundred female students each year.

IBM also redesigned the career section of its website to provide interviews with senior female leaders and offer specific female-oriented advice about seeking a career at IBM.

They applied flexible working across the board to every job at every level, including job sharing, home working and reduced hours, and working a compressed week. To add to their family-friendly policies, they also provide access to emergency childcare and eldercare providers for employees who might need this temporary support.

For employees on maternity leave, they operate an online community where women can stay connected and find a 'buddy' to support them when they return to work. Fathers are also connected with help, advice, and support in a similar manner.

They also operate a reverse mentoring program, where employees from minority groups share experiences with senior leaders. This keeps the senior leaders in touch with the experiences of lower-level employees and gives those employees direct access to senior leadership.

In recognition of their gender diversity initiatives, IBM was awarded the prestigious Catalyst award in 2018.

So far, in this book, we've focused mostly on women in

established organizations and how they can climb the corporate ladder. However, not all female leaders are taking the more conventional approach. A growing number of women are taking the plunge into entrepreneurship.

In the next chapter, we'll investigate how women are taking the lead by starting their own businesses and creating big change.

Chapter 8 – The Rise and Rise of the Female Entrepreneur

"There is no better personal development tool than running your own business."
Ali Brown, Entrepreneurial Guru for Women.

How Women Are Leveraging Their Strengths In Entrepreneurial Endeavors

When we think of entrepreneurs, most people think of one of the many successful male entrepreneurs like Jeff Bezos, Mark Zuckerberg, or Tim Ferriss.

For a long time, entrepreneurship was a male-dominated territory. The average entrepreneur is in their thirties, at which time a lot of women are busy raising children whilst also potentially working to contribute to household finances. Given that becoming an entrepreneur can involve very long hours and unpredictable income, leaping into entrepreneurship might not even be on women's radar at that time.

However, with the rise of online technology and a surge of interest in gender equality, we're seeing more and more female entrepreneurs. According to the National Association of Women Business Owners, there are over 9 million U.S companies owned by women. These women-owned companies employ over 7 million people and generate approximately $1.5 billion in sales.

Over the last several years there's been a rise in the number of women choosing to set up their own businesses to give them the income and flexibility they need. It's even brought the term 'Mompreneur' into common usage.

So, what's driving more and more women to entrepreneurship? Issues like the ones we've discussed in earlier chapters, like lack of flexible working options and pay disparity have prompted many women to take matters into their own hands. What better way to tackle the issue than to create your own ideal working conditions?

However is entrepreneurship the best way for women to lead the way for positive change?

Female Entrepreneurs Work Differently

In the same way that female leaders, in general, have a different leadership approach than most of their male colleagues, female entrepreneurs do things differently.

On the whole, female entrepreneurs have less ambitious growth aspirations and hire fewer people. This has, in the past, led people to believe that women entrepreneurs were less serious, committed or successful.

Yet that's not the whole picture. A Dow Jones study into U.S venture-backed companies uncovered that the successful companies had twice as many women founders or co-founders. Further research from financial institutions has shown that business loans granted to female founders are less risky and result in fewer write-offs. These findings indicate that by and large, women-owned businesses are more stable and secure.

Women are also more likely to start charitable ventures or businesses with a social/ethical slant to them. There's even a term among some entrepreneurs who consider themselves 'heart-centered'. This means that they run businesses who aren't just about profit – they're about giving something back in some way. Most people who identify as heart-centered entrepreneurs are women.

High Profile Women Entrepreneurs & The Lessons We Can Take

There's some evidence to suggest that female entrepreneurs don't have goals as aggressive as their male counterparts. However, that doesn't mean there aren't plenty of highly successful female entrepreneurs.

Let's take a look at some of the female entrepreneurs who've broken the mold and found great success in many areas, from fashion to health.

Jo Malone: Jo Malone London, Jo Loves

Jo Malone is a UK entrepreneur who founded a global brand, *Jo Malone London*, in 1994 along with her mother, Eileen. She later sold it in 2006 to *Estee Lauder* for an undisclosed amount supposed to be in the millions. In 2011, she founded a new fragrance company, *Jo Loves*.

Jo grew up in social housing in the Bexley Heath area of Kent, a far cry from the upmarket streets that her stores would eventually grace. Starting her career as a facialist, she quickly discovered that she had a talent for mixing fragrances for her homemade beauty products.

Originally selling and gifting her products to customers of her facialist business, she found that she was getting large amounts of repeat orders. She eventually founded *Jo Malone London* to sell them to a wider audience.

Sophia Amoruso: Nasty Gal, Girlboss Media

Sophia Amoruso started her eBay store Nasty Gal Vintage at age 22. She sourced vintage clothing and other items, mostly from thrift stores and resold them at a profit on her eBay store.

In 2008, Sophia left eBay and launched her Nasty Gal retail website.

Amoruso developed a big social media following, which helped propel Nasty Gal on to further success. In 2016 she was listed in Forbes as one of the richest self-made women in the world.
In 2014, she published her autobiography *#GIRLBOSS*, which was later adapted into a Netflix show, Girlboss.

Unfortunately, Nasty Gal ended up filing for bankruptcy shortly after Amoruso stepped down as CEO. It was purchased by the Boohoo Group in 2017 for $20 million.

After the sale of Nasty Gal, Amoruso leveraged her experience as a female leader and her autobiography success to launch Girlboss Media. Girlboss describes itself as, *"a community of strong, curious, and ambitious women redefining success on our own terms."*

Anne Wojcicki: 23andMe

Anne Wojcicki co-founded the human genome research company 23andMe with Linda Avey in 2006. The company name is a reference to the 23 pairs of chromosomes found in a normal human cell. In 2008 their test kit was named the Invention of the Year by Time Magazine.

In 2015 the company gained FDA approval for health-related tests, and in 2018 they began collaboration with

GlaxoSmithKline to develop new medicines from the results of their tests.

High-profile female leaderships seems to run in the family, as her sister, Susan Wojcicki, is the CEO of YouTube

Arianna Huffington: The Huffington Post, Thrive Global
Ariana Huffington co-founded The Huffington Post in 2005 and has an estimated net worth of $50 million. AOL purchased The Huffington Post in 2011 for over $300 million, with Ariana Huffington remaining on board as company president.

Her ex-husband Michael was a politician, and Arianna was quite active in political circles, helping her husband campaign and voicing her own political views. In 2003, she ran against Arnold Schwarzenegger for the California governorship but withdrew from campaigning before the election.

In 2016, Huffington stood down as CEO of The Huffington Post to start a new business, Thrive Global which promotes wellbeing.

She's also the internationally bestselling author of books including *Thrive: The Third Metric to Redefining Success and Creating a Life of Well-Being, Wisdom, and Wonder* and *The Sleep Revolution: Transforming Your Life, One Night At A Time*

Jasmine Crowe: BCG, Goodr
Jasmine Crowe launched her first business, Black Celebrity Giving (BCG) in 2011. BCG was created to highlight, celebrate and support black people doing positive things to impact communities.

In 2017, Jasmine founded her second company Goodr. Goodr uses technology to manage surplus food waste from restaurants and distribute it to the people who needed it most. Goodr allows businesses to register the donations as tax-deductible charity donations – allowing both the business and the recipients to benefit.

Sara Blakely: SPANX

Sarah Blakely came up with the idea for Spanx while working in a sales role for an office supply company. She was inspired by the way the control-top hosiery she wore for work gave a smoother figure. She wanted to recreate that look with a variety of clothing without the need for wearing full hosiery.

She spent two years and all of her $5,000 life savings developing the product. Initially, her product was rejected by hosiery mills, which Blakely noted were mostly owned and run by men who had no experience of being an end-user. Eventually, one of the male owners was encouraged by his daughters to support Blakely's product and a prototype was eventually created.

When Spanx was named one of Oprah Winfrey's Favorite Things, the business took off. Since then, Blakely has been featured on numerous 'Top 100' lists, including Time Magazine and Forbes.

In 2006, she launched the Sara Blakely Foundation, a non-profit organization to help support women through education and entrepreneurial training.

Emily Weiss: Glossier

Emily Weiss launched a beauty blog, Into the Gloss late in 2010, while working as an on-set styling assistant for

Vogue. Into the Gloss did so well that she eventually left her job at Vogue to focus on the blog and related ventures.

In 2013, she began approaching venture capitalists to raise funds for expansion into e-commerce. Glossier was launched in October 2014 with just four beauty products. It has since expanded the range to over six product categories, including Glossiwear, a clothing and accessories range. Glossier was valued at $1.2 billion in March 2019.

Industries That Fit Well with Feminine Skills

As you can see, lots of women have found entrepreneurial success by creating products for women to fill a gap in the market, like Sarah Blakely and Emily Weiss.

Alongside some of the more traditional industries that attract women to create their own businesses – beauty salons, boutiques, hairdressers, etc., more and more women are creating businesses in previously male-dominated industries.

Women are starting to more frequently get into areas like disruptive tech. For example, Jasmine Crowe and Goodr, and often these female-led startups are driven as much by social conscience as by profit.

Women, in general, are well-suited to industries like health and wellbeing, education, and retail. Often when asked, women will say they felt almost 'called' to one of the more feminine industries.

It's important to point out that there is no more or less value in any industry. The key ingredient for most successful entrepreneurs is passion. Is it something you feel passionately about and is it something you can create a business from? If so, then it's got great potential regardless of whether it's flattering undergarments or industry-disrupting software that you're developing.

The crucial message is that women are taking charge and building businesses that ignite their passion. Entrepreneurship gives them the opportunity to drive change by creating companies that are female-led and female-friendly at all levels.

Then there's the fact that some of the more feminine skills are valuable in absolutely any industry. Some of the skills that make female entrepreneurs stand out in male-dominated STEM industries are:

- **Great negotiation skills.** The collaborative approach that comes naturally to a lot of women is an asset when it comes to high-level negotiating.
- **Emotional Intelligence.** The emotional intelligence that most women have comes in handy for everything from identifying what will resonate with your target client to how to manage business relationships.
- **Listening skills.** Women tend to make good listeners, and that can help them identify where they need to make changes based on feedback. It can also help them connect with clients, business partners, and potential investors.

There's no single industry that's better for women to start a business in. If you have the drive and passion, there are no limits!

Building an Effective Online Business

It can be daunting to take that leap into entrepreneurship, especially if you don't have a lot of cash to invest in your new endeavor. Network marketing has, for many years, been the most accessible low-entry-cost option for women who need flexibility and the freedom to be their own boss.

However, the online business world is booming, and work from home/be your own boss opportunities are not limited to network marketing. If you love network marketing and you enjoy building a team, then that's still one option. Many network marketing companies are designed to attract women, and they push the 'working stay at home mom' angle.

However, there are almost endless options for people of any gender to start up an online business with little or no outlay. If you have a business idea, you're one step closer to being your own boss.

Many of the most successful entrepreneurs spotted a gap in the market for a product and service and then provided it. However, there's also success to be had by doing something better than everyone else, or by providing an existing service in a new or better way for a certain target market.

If you have your heart set on inventing or producing a product and don't have a big budget, there are even crowdfunding websites like Kickstarter. These allow you to can gauge public interest as well as raise the funds you need.

There are a lot of ways that you can create your own business with little or no budget. Take NastyGal's founder, Sophia Amoruso. She began her business selling vintage clothing on eBay. She'd visit thrift stores, find classic designer items that the store staff had completely undervalued, snap them up, and then sell them on at a higher price.

There are so many options for starting your own business and they don't all involve selling a product. You can market a skill you have as a service. Lots of women enter into online coaching because their feminine skills like listening and communication tend to make them good coaches. Other popular options are freelance writer, editor, web designer, social media manager, or virtual assistant.

For no initial outlay at all, depending on what you choose, you can market your skills on freelancing sites or use social media to spread the word about your services.

If you want to sell a product with little to no outlay, you can dropship. There are even services where you can design T-Shirts and other easily printed items like mugs and cushions. You then sell them via the service, who prints and ships them on demand.

Of course, there are some considerations. You'll need to have command of the skills that you want to charge people for. You'll also need to investigate if you need any kind of indemnity insurance. There may be specific qualifications or regulatory requirements for your business in the countries you want to operate in. None of that is as difficult as it sounds. However, becoming your own boss isn't always easy.

Overcoming the Challenges of Starting your own Business

To run a successful business – whatever your definition of success – you, first of all, need to believe that you can do it. The same lack of confidence that stops women applying for jobs when they don't match the role 100% can stop women from believing they have what it takes to become an entrepreneur.

Even once you believe you can do it, there are practical considerations to factor in. If your business needs funding, you may need to raise venture capital, which can be a long and arduous process.

If you're starting small scale and low budget, you may not need to worry about investors, but you will need to find clients and customers. If you've never needed to do this before it can be very daunting.

Almost all business owners experience periods of financial and emotional difficulty as they navigate the waters of self-employment. You're free of many of the constraints of the formal corporate world but becoming a business owner brings many of its own challenges.

Why The Challenges Of Female Entrepreneurship Are Worth It

Women are increasingly becoming entrepreneurs – and they're increasingly very successful at it. According to one survey by Smallbiztrends.com, over half of female entrepreneurs expected their incomes to increase in 2018. This was on a level with the number of males who also felt their income would increase.

Over the last decade, businesses owned by women have

grown at a 1.5 times greater rate than other small businesses. The tides are beginning to turn in a big way towards female entrepreneurship.

Then there's the flexibility and freedom that comes with being your own boss. While it might not come easily at first, once you've built a client base, you are effectively in complete control. Your income is completely linked to your own performance, and you can work the hours you choose. Even better, your own business never comes with a glass ceiling because you're starting right at the top.

Building A Business That Nurtures And Supports Other Women

The other great thing about becoming your own boss and building a business is that you can nurture and support other women. Your entire business can be built around nurturing and supporting other women by becoming a coach, or by creating products that are designed for women.

Yet any business can support and nurture women by hiring other women, joining networking groups, and offering advice or training to other women.

With female-owned businesses employing over 7 million people in the U.S, their contribution to the economy is impressive. Even better, female entrepreneurs are in the unique position of being able to implement female-friendly working practices from day one.

As many women start businesses in the hope that they will be able to achieve a proper work-life balance, that ethos remains when they are ready to hire their first employees. As such, female entrepreneurs know that women with caring responsibilities are perfectly capable of achieving the same work to the same standard as a male employee.

Even by simply being a female business owner, you're a powerful role model for other women. By recognizing that and aiming to support and inspire other women to achieve the same, female entrepreneurs can make a huge contribution to gender diversity.

There are lots of ways that women can become leaders, right down to taking the matter into their own hands and forming their own businesses. There's lots that we can all do to keep pushing forward and leading the way towards gender diversity.

One of the ways we can make things better for the future is to start to nurture young women and girls early in their educational journey. In the next chapter, we'll look at what can be done to develop the female leaders of tomorrow and make their path a little clearer.

Chapter 9 – Nurturing The Next Generation Of Female Leaders

"I love to see a young girl go out and grab the world by the lapels. Life's a bitch. You've got to go out and kick ass."
Maya Angelou, American poet, singer, memoirist, and civil rights activist.

There's a lot that working women can do to help encourage gender diversity in their workplaces. However, to work against the biases that currently exist we need to start addressing the issues early on.

Starting to prepare young leaders of all genders while they are in high school can help to redefine the next generation's idea of what a great leader looks like. It can even help us remove gender from the equation.

Combatting Gender Bias Fast

"Don't let anyone rob you of your imagination, your creativity, or your curiosity. It's your place in the world; it's your life."
Dr. Mae Jemison, Engineer, physician, and NASA astronaut.

Numerous studies are showing that female students are encouraged down different paths to male students quite early in their education. To combat this, high schools should review their career guidance policies to remove gender biases.

Another factor that can have an impact on how young

people view leadership and gender is the lack of female leaders in high schools. Women are underrepresented across educational leadership in the same way they are underrepresented across the private sector and government.

Girls and young women need to have role models to look to and imagine that they could achieve similar things. With a lack of obvious female leader role models in the school system, it's even more important that the curriculum addresses the topic. How can this be done?

High school is a particularly relevant time to tackle the gender biases that are hidden in the school system. It's well known that adolescence is a difficult time, and it's a time when children begin to really feel the weight of societal gender norms.

As we've discussed earlier, they will have been aware of these norms since pre-school and before. However, they can begin to heavily affect the choices girls make and the aspirations they have during high school.

Several studies have confirmed that the notion of males as assertive and females as passive is reinforced in classrooms. Males will often dominate any discussion in the classroom and volunteer their opinions freely. Female students, on the other hand, tend to be less willing to put themselves forward.

This difference in behavior leads to teachers unconsciously tending to request input from male students more than female ones. This means that girls rarely speak up in class – a behavior that then carries across into other mixed-gender environments and is eventually demonstrated in the workplace as a reluctance to speak up.

After thousands of observation hours in various classrooms and grade levels, the research team behind the book, *Still Failing at Fairness: How Gender Bias Cheats Girls and Boys in School and What We Can Do About It*, found that the amount of gender bias in lessons and teaching practices, in their words was 'startling'. Their study unearthed that teachers asked female students fewer questions than male students and frequently provided males with more feedback.

However, stereotype reinforcement doesn't stop there. The teaching materials used to deliver the curriculum often demonstrate gender bias. Textbook authors are predominantly male, and characterizations in teaching materials are frequently male, and frequently adhere to gender stereotypes.

Several UNESCO studies found that women were underrepresented in numerous texts, and many contain stereotypes or even offensive comments about women.

To eradicate gender bias, the teaching materials used in high schools need to represent genders equally, and not attach stereotypes to them. For example, textbooks should contain strong female role models as well as male ones and describe their achievements in a non-gendered way. When this is the case, we'll be one step closer to raising a generation of people that aren't plagued by unconscious biases.

Changing the content of educational materials will take time and funds that not all schools have access to. Teachers can help speed the process up by identifying and calling out gender biases in their educational materials. They can also ensure that they call on the opinions of their female students as frequently as the male ones.

Mentoring Programs

One way to encourage leadership skills in young women is to connect them with mentors early in their careers. Mentors can even be employed during high school and college to help advise and guide students through the various choices that can impact their future career.

There are existing organizations that mentor girls and young women, often in underprivileged communities where their support is needed the most.

These organizations connect young women with mentors who encourage their ambition, help them set and achieve goals, and boost their confidence. Some are working with specialist industries like STEM subjects, journalism, and tech to encourage more young women to pursue roles in these industries.

Organizations like these are crucial for empowering and inspiring our next generation of female leaders.

Even in locations where these organizations aren't accessible, or for more general mentoring, there are ways that teachers and female leaders in the community can help. We often think of mentoring as a completely 1-1 relationship, and 1-1 is indeed the most common, ideal method.

However, group mentoring is also a valuable resource for young women who may not be able to access other support. With group mentoring, it only takes one champion willing to lead the sessions, and they can invite other female leaders to share their knowledge and experience in sessions. By allowing young women to discuss the challenges and rewards of leadership with a real female leader, they can understand what's possible to achieve in their own lives.

Group mentoring is a very flexible and adaptable way to give young women access to the support they need. Beyond providing role models, mentoring allows young women to start to develop the real-life skills that they'll need to become future leaders.

Skills like communication, negotiation, stakeholder management, and collaboration can all be learned in a mentoring environment. Not only will developing these skills stand young women in good stead for their future careers but it will also boost their self-esteem too.

Real Life Case Study of Mentorship and Support

The Young Women Leaders Program (YWLP) at the University of Virginia has been successfully running for over 20 years. It employs both group mentoring and individual mentoring to encourage young future female leaders.

They have linked with four local area middle schools, who each nominate girls that they believe would benefit from the program. Those girls are then matched with individual mentors from the college as well as allocated a group for weekly two-hour sessions that continue for a year.

As well as their individual mentors attending group sessions with them, once a week, participants meet with their personal mentor for one-on-one support. The group sessions focus on problem-solving, decision making and developing leadership skills in the girls.

Discussion, prompts and activities help the groups engage with the topics presented.

The program has the added benefit of being located on a university campus, allowing the participants some exposure to this type of environment. For some of the girls, it may be the first time that they've considered attending a college after high school.

The results of the program are impressive. An evaluation revealed that over three-quarters of the participants stated that the program helped them:

- improve the way they listen to people with views different from their own,
- support and talk with their friends,
- deal with their problems,
- communicate with other kids at school,
- interact with people who are different from them,
- think about their future.

Over two-thirds reported that the program helped them improve their self-esteem, get involved in school as a leader, make decisions about their behavior at school, and deal with difficult situations.

Investing in women's leadership, starting in schools, has the power to bring about widespread change. It's not a short-term solution but a commitment to the future. Investing in young women's leadership will not only change the trajectory of their future but that of the entire business world as well.

Conclusion: Be Strong, Lead, Find Success

"How wonderful it is that nobody need wait a single moment before starting to improve the world."
Anne Frank, German diarist.

Despite the differences in male and female leadership styles, both men and women can make incredibly effective leaders. The differences are apparent in various studies but the percentages are small. Additionally, all of the research only demonstrates averages, and there is a vast variance among individuals.

Leadership ability is rarely about the gender of the leader and is more about the individual. However, our innate unconscious gender biases and social expectations can cause us to view male and female leaders differently. It's those biases and societal expectations that need to be addressed so that we can all move forward into a more gender-diverse future.

The burden of changing the way we think about women in leadership falls to all of us. By dispassionately identifying when we're allowing gender bias to influence the way we perceive other people, we can become aware when it is happening and take steps to change our perceptions.

The good news is that change is happening and it's happening at a fast rate. Women's issues are getting more and more media coverage, and fewer women and men are willing to tolerate unfairness in the workplace.

To challenge gender discrimination, there are lots of things you can do. To recap, here are some positive actions that we can all take in the workplace.

Speak Up

"It took me quite a long time to develop a voice, and now that I have it, I am not going to be silent."
Madeleine Albright, Former U.S. Secretary of State.

Share your opinions and your ambitions freely. Showing up and working hard is essential but giving yourself the best chance of moving up the corporate ladder means you'll need to be heard.

Be your own advocate, and seek out a sponsor who can also speak up on your behalf. Make it clear to your managers and colleagues exactly what you bring to the table and why it's valuable.

Keep Learning
Invest in learning how to be the best at your role. Back up your opinions with facts and data when possible to lend your arguments extra credibility. Take an interest in the overall business goals and strategy and figure out how your ambitions align with the company.

Keep in touch with developments in your industry, and have conversations with your colleagues and superiors about them. Doing this demonstrates your commitment to the organization's success, as well as showing that you have the commercial knowledge and understanding to make significant leadership decisions that take the broader context into account. In short, work towards making yourself an invaluable expert!

Seek Out Mentors And Sponsors
Mentors and sponsors have different roles to play in your career progression but they're both incredibly valuable.

Take advantage of any programs in your workplace designed to link you with a mentor or a sponsor.

If your workplace doesn't have a program, seek them out yourself. Mentors can even be external to your organization. Any mentor should have experience and knowledge that would be directly relevant to your role or the role that you consider to be your next step.

Recognize Your Achievements And Strengths

Don't allow perfectionism or self-confidence issues to hold you back. Keep a note of your achievements and celebrate them. From academic certifications to landing a new client for your organization, make sure that you recognize the value and knowledge that you have.

Take chances and put yourself out there. Apply for a role you want even if you don't meet 100% of the criteria. When you see an opportunity, take it.

Embrace Your Femininity

Allow yourself to express your opinions and handle situations in a way that makes the best use of your strengths. When those strengths are traits that are perceived as feminine, embrace that. Don't try to fit a mold made for somebody else.

Don't try too hard to emulate more masculine traits if those don't come naturally. Forcing yourself to behave in a way that's not natural simply to appear more like 'leadership material' can make you feel miserable and can also have the opposite effect.

You're already leadership material. Anyone can learn the skills it takes to be a leader but to do it well, you need to work with your natural personality traits. By trying to force masculine behaviors, you're reinforcing the message to yourself and to everyone else that only masculine traits are leadership traits.

Instead of the 'if you can't beat them join them' approach, remember that you're a role model for other aspiring leaders. Demonstrate to them – and yourself – that women are already competent and effective leaders.

With continued perseverance, we can all contribute to the movement towards gender equality. The ultimate goal is to live and work in a world where men and women are honestly considered equal in their social roles.

To get there, we need to work together, to challenge outdated gender stereotypes that currently hold so many people back. Now go out there and change the world!

"If the first woman God ever made was strong enough to turn the world upside down all alone, these women together ought to be able to turn it back, and get it right side up again! And now they is asking to do it, the men better let them."
Sojourner Truth, American abolitionist.

Printed in Great Britain
by Amazon